PLAN TO PROFIT

Business Planning for Builders and Remodelers

CHUCK MILLER

ISBN 978-1-961017-85-6 (Paperback)
ISBN 978-1-961017-87-0 (Hardback)
ISBN 978-1-961017-86-3 (Ebook)

Inquiries and Book Orders should be addressed to:

Leavitt Peak Press
17901 Pioneer Blvd Ste L #298, Artesia, California 90701
Phone #: 2092191548

PLAN TO PROFIT: A BUSINESS PLAN BLUEPRINT FOR BUILDERS AND REMODELERS

Small businesses in the construction industry have the second highest failure rate of businesses in any industry. A survey of builder and remodeler members of the National Association of Home Builders revealed that fewer than 12% had a written business plan, fewer than 15% had written operating budgets, less than 18% had written mission statements, and almost 70% had no formal planning procedures.

Your business plan is the most important management tool you have. It defines your strategy, tactics, and specific activities for execution, including dates and deadlines, budgets and cash flow. It will guide you regarding the types of projects to pursue, how you market your company, the people to hire and the funding needed to succeed. Planning establishes your short-term, intermediate-term, and long-term goals and outlines how you can achieve those goals by breaking down long-range plans into manageable short-term goals that everyone on your team can identify and support.

Your business plan will help you focus strategy, manage milestones, manage metrics, assign and track responsibilities and performance, and manage money using projections for sales, costs, expenses, and cash.

Plan To Profit provides a blueprint you can follow to develop a working business plan. It walks you step by step through the process, starting with market research and analysis, followed by developing your product and service, marketing and sales, operations, leadership team and staffing, and goals and action plans. It guides you in creating your financial forecasts and budgets; your vision, mission, core values; and your unique selling proposition. It includes a Microsoft® Excel® workbook which contains financial statement worksheets that you can use to complete your pro forma financial statements.

CONTENTS

ABOUT THE AUTHOR

Chuck Miller is Owner of Chuck Miller Consulting LLC, Chuck Miller Education Services LLC, and Chuck Miller Construction Inc.

He began his career in 1968 as an apprentice carpenter. He has managed several building companies and supervised the construction of single and multi-family residential, commercial, and institutional projects across the United States.

He is an active member and Life Director of the National Association of Home Builders (NAHB), the Building Contractors Association of Southwestern Idaho (BCASWI), and Idaho Building Contractors Association (IBCA).

He was recognized by the BCASWI as their 2003 Builder of the Year and by the IBCA as their 2017 Builder of the Year for his service to the association, the building industry, and the community.

Chuck has earned eleven (11) NAHB professional designations:

- Graduate Master Builder (GMB)
- Graduate Master Remodeler (GMR)
- Certified Graduate Builder (CGB)
- Certified Graduate Remodeler (CGR)
- Certified Aging-In-Place Specialist (CAPS)
- Master Certified Green Professional (MCGP)
- Certified Green Professional (CGP)
- Master In Residential Marketing (MIRM)
- Certified New Home Marketing Professional (CMP)
- Master Certified New Home Sales Professional (MCSP) and
- Certified New Home Sales Professional (CSP)

He was named the NAHB 2017 Builder Designee of the Year for his commitment to earning and promoting NAHB's professional designations. He was previously named the 2015 Master in Residential Marketing of the Year and the 2009 Certified Graduate Builder of the Year.

He became an instructor for the NAHB in 1999 and is a licensed provider of NAHB education programs. He is a Master Instructor for NAHB courses and was named NAHB's 2016 Sales and Marketing/IRM Educator of the Year.

Chuck was the Principal Writer for NAHB's The Project Schedule as a Planning and Communication Tool course. He has also served as a Subject Matter Expert on several NAHB course revisions including

- Principles of Residential Marketing: Research and Analysis
- Principles of Residential Marketing: Strategy and Implementation
- Marketing and Sales for Building Professionals
- Estimating and Scheduling for Profitable Business Operations

- House Construction As A Selling Tool
- Builder Assessment Review (BAR) exam

Since becoming a licensed provider for NAHB Education courses, he has worked to bring NAHB's courses to the Realtor community in Idaho and to the other local associations who do not hold licenses.

He has presented NAHB's "Homes of Our Own" programs created by NAHB to teach chil- dren, young adults, parents, and teachers about home building, environmental issues, and careers in home building industries.

In addition to being a Master Instructor for NAHB, he is also a National Center for Construction Education and Research Certified Carpentry Instructor and an instructor for the National Endowment for Financial Education® (NEFE®) High School Financial Planning Program® (HSFPP), a nationally known money management program for high school students.

He serves on the Ada County Building Code Board of Appeals.

He is a graduate of Western Illinois University, where he majored in Construction Technology and minored in Real Estate and Business Management. He is also a Dale Carnegie graduate.

ACKNOWLEDGEMENTS

"No one who achieves success does so without acknowledging the help of others. The wise and confident acknowledge this help with gratitude."

—Alfred North Whitehead

This book is a combination of the knowledge I've gained through my own experiences managing small building companies, through professional designation courses I've taken with dedicated and knowledgeable instructors – mostly National Association of Home Builders (NAHB) professional designation courses – and from friends, mentors, and colleagues in the industry.

I'd like to acknowledge my friends and mentors:

Bonnie Alfriend, who introduced me to NAHB's Institute of Residential Marketing (IRM) and who taught my first IRM class – Certified New Home Sales Professional.

Roger Fiehn. Roger passed away on November 4, 2013. Roger was a custom builder and real estate broker and the most active and highly rated faculty member of NAHB's education program. Roger was always available to share his knowledge and strategize ways to help me achieve my career goals. In addition to being my instructor for several IRM courses, he mentored me in writing my Master In Residential Marketing Case Study, reviewing each section I wrote and offering comments and suggestions.

S. Robert August, one of the most distinguished, award-winning marketing, management, and sales strategists in the world today. Robert specializes in management, marketing, and sales consult- ing in the real estate industry and beyond. Robert has been honored twice by NAHB's National Sales and Marketing Council with the William "Bill" Molster Award, given to the most outstand- ing sales and marketing professional in the nation. Robert is the only recipient to win the Molster Award twice (1996, 2002). Robert most recent awards include the Legend of Residential Marketing (2017); the NAHB Sales and Marketing Educator of the Year (2015); and Master Certified Sales Professional of the Year (2014). Robert is always available to answer my questions and offer advice.

Members of NAHB who I have had the privilege of working with as a subject matter expert on a number NAHB course re-writes - Tom Stephanie, John Barrows, Paul Sullivan, CAPS, CGP, CGR; Steve Black; Vince Napolitano; Dianne D. Beaton, CAPS, CGA; Tim Shigley, CAPS, CGP, CGR, GMB, GMR; Robert Criner, CAPS, CGB, CGP, CGR, GMB, GMR; Tony Foust, CAPS, CGB, CGP; John Barrows, CGB, CGP, GMB, MCGP; Jim Carr, CGP, GMB; Alan Hanbury, Jr., APS, CGP, CGR, GMR; Gaye Burwell Orr, CMP, MIRM; Jean L. Ewell, CAASH, CMP, CSP, Master CSP, MIRM; Tammie Smoot, CMP, CSP, Master CSP, MIRM; Kristy Yule, CMP, MIRM; Charles Graham, CMP, MIRM; Meredith Oliver, CMP, CSP, Master CSP, MIRM; Skip Howes, CAPS, CGB, CGP; Mitch Levinson, CAPS, CGP, CMP, CSP, MIRM; and Brian Flook, CMP, MIRM.

Members of NAHB and fellow authors whose books have contributed to my knowledge and several of which were used as resources in writing this book: Meredith Oliver, Mitch Levinson, Carol Morgan, Brian Flook, and Ken Brookings.

Thanks to my daughter, Lindsay Miller, for editing the manuscript.

Zig Ziglar said "All one needs to do is read - books, magazines, research the Internet - and pay attention to the influencers in their lives to discover the myriad people of strong moral character who have and still are making positive, meaningful contributions and differences in our world." Without reading and paying attention to what you have all taught me over the years, I never would have been able to write this book. My hope is that this book will make a positive, meaningful con- tribution and difference in the world – at least in the world of building and remodeling.

INTRODUCTION

"You don't have to be a genius or a visionary or even a college graduate to be successful. You just need a framework and a dream."

—Michael Dell

There are a million reasons not to go into business: starting a business takes an insane amount of time; it's risky; it can destroy your life; you might go into debt; when you fail, it's public and per- sonal; and the list goes on. But even with all these uncertainties, people are still attracted to starting their own businesses...to earn a living, provide for their families and fulfill their own dreams. In fact, between March 2014 and March 2015, just over 679,000 new businesses were started in the United States.

If you do a Google search of "Why Small Businesses Fail," it will return approximately 10 mil- lion results. Numerous reasons are cited, but common causes include ineffective marketing, being out of touch with clients, lack of differentiation in the market, overconfidence, burnout, underesti- mating the compe- tition, overgeneralization, poor pricing strategy, failure to price their product or service correctly, failure to adequately anticipate cash flow, poor financial management, believing you can do everything yourself, rapid growth, and failure to communicate value propositions in clear, concise and compelling fashion.

The Bureau of Labor Statistics' most recent data shows that 20.1% of small businesses that opened in March of 2015 failed within one year. Only about half of all establishments survive five years or longer.

According to the Small Business Development Center, nine out of ten business failures in the United States are caused by a lack of planning and general business management skills. I believe that most, if not all, these common causes could be prevented by having a well thought-out, well-written business plan. A written business plan forces business owners to assess their business management knowledge and skills. It provides the framework for success that Michael Dell refers to.

For small businesses in the construction industry, about 25% of businesses fail their first year, 35% fail in their second year, and about 65% fail within their first five years - the second highest failure rate of all industries. These rates are relatively consistent over time, suggesting that year-over- year economic factors don't have much of an impact on small business failure rates. The construc- tion industry in the United States is made up of nearly 700,000 large and small companies, includ- ing subcontractors. These compa- nies employ approximately 7,000,000 workers. Gross Domestic Product from construction in the United States averaged $641.99 Billion from 2005 until 2016, reaching an all-time high of $784.90 billion or 4.2 percent of GDP in the third quarter of 2016. Of these 700,000 construction companies in the United States, more than 171,000 are residential homebuilding and remodeling companies. According to the U.S. Department of Commerce Bureau of Economic Analysis, residential construction accounted for 3.8 percent of the country's gross domestic product. The value of new residential construction put in place by residential home builders and home builders was $233.7 billion in the 3rd quarter of 2016, and small-volume home-builders make up the majority of residential construction companies. According to the National Association of Home Builders, 70 percent of its membership produces 25 homes or fewer per year (NAHB, 2006). The residential construction industry is important to the financial health of the nation.

A survey of builder and remodeler members of the National Association of Home Builders (NAHB) revealed that fewer than 12 percent had a written business plan, fewer than 15 percent had written operating budgets, less than 18 percent had written mission statements, and almost 70 percent of respondents had no formal planning procedures.

Would you build or remodel without a plan? How about a budget? Would you start building or remodeling a home without a budget estimate? How about a schedule? Would you build or remodel a house without a schedule? No. So, why would you try to build and manage a business without a written plan, without an operating budget, and without a formal planning procedure? Amazon has over 78,000 books on business planning and 371 specifically on how to write a business plan. NAHB's Builder Books lists 9 books under the category Business Planning but only one is a guide to developing a business plan and it is currently only available on Amazon.com as a used book.

This book is written by a builder and remodeler specifically for builders and remodelers. It is written specifically for the small volume builder or remodeler who typically wears many hats - president, marketing director, operations manager, project manager, human resource director, accountant, and everything in between. It discusses the different functions within your company, provides information and guidance, and walks you step-by-step through writing your business plan. It even includes a Standard Business Plan template as a Microsoft® Word® document so you can write each section of your business plan as you complete each chapter of the book. And it comes with Pro Forma Financial Statement templates in a Microsoft® Excel® workbook that you can fill-in with your data.

It is my hope that the business plan you develop by completing the steps in this book will become your most important tool, that implementing your plan will guarantee that you are one of the small businesses in the construction industry that survives and thrives beyond 5 years, and that this book will increase the five year survival rate for small businesses in the construction industry.

CHAPTER 1

WHAT IS A BUSINESS PLAN?

"A business plan is a blueprint for a profitable business."

—Vocabulary.com Dictionary

In its simplest form, a business plan is the blueprint for your business that outlines goals and details how you plan to achieve those goals. Every business should have long-term and short-term goals, sales targets, and expense budgets—a business plan encompasses all of those things.

It is a blueprint of how your business is going to work; and how you're going to make it succeed. Business plans are not just for starting a new business or applying for business loans. Business plans are also vital for running a business, whether or not it needs new loans or new investments. Existing businesses should have business plans they maintain and update as market conditions change and as new opportunities arise.

The task of writing a business plan today is much less daunting than it used to be. These days, business plans are simpler, shorter, and easier to produce than they have ever been. Gone are the days of 30- and 40-page business plans; modern business plans are shorter, easier to write, and easier to read.

Business plans come in many different forms and can differ greatly in length, detail, and presentation. They can either be internal or external, i.e. the standard business plan document. The elements of a standard business plan include:

- Executive Summary
- Vision, Mission, Core Values, and Unique Selling Proposition
- Company Overview
- Market Analysis
- Product And Service Plan
- Marketing and Sales Plan
- Operations Plan
- The Leadership Team And Staffing Plan
- Goals and Action Plans
- Financial Forecasts And Budgets
- Review Schedule
- Supporting Data Exhibits

Think of your business plan as a checklist of all the things you need to consider in order to build a successful business. It doesn't have to be a long, formal document. Use the above as a check- list, but don't include anything that doesn't have a purpose in your business. `

Internal business plans are management tools used to guide the operation and growth of both startups and existing businesses. They help business owners think through strategic decisions and measure progress towards goals.

An internal business plan focuses on market analysis, your marketing and sales plan, financial forecasts and budgets, operations, and goals, but can skip details about company history and the leadership team, since everyone in the company almost certainly knows this information.

External business plans - the formal business plan documents -can also be a management tool but are designed to be read by outsiders to provide information about a business.

If you are approaching a banker for a loan for a startup business, your loan officer may suggest a Small Business Administration (SBA) loan, which will require a written business plan. If you have an existing business and are approaching a bank for capital to expand the business, they might not require a business plan, but they may look more favorably on your application if you have one.

A formal business plan document is an extension of the internal business plan. But while an internal plan is short on polish and formality, a formal business plan document should be very well-presented, with more attention to detail in the language and format. In addition, an external plan details how potential funds are going to be used. Finally, external plans put a strong emphasis on the team that is building the company and include biographies of key team members and how their background and experience is going to help grow the company.

Regardless of the audience, business plans should be dynamic documents subject to constant change. In all cases, the most important section of the business plan is the review schedule. Just writing a business plan does not guarantee your success. The best way to extract value from your business plan is to use it as an ongoing management tool. It must be constantly revisited and revised to reflect current conditions and the new information you've collected as you run your business.

Now that you have an overview of what a business plan is, you might be asking *"Why do I need a business plan?"* We'll discuss that in the next chapter.

CHAPTER 2

WHY DO I NEED A BUSINESS PLAN?

"If you fail to plan, you are planning to fail!"

—Benjamin Franklin

A business plan provides a blueprint for managing your building or remodeling company. Blueprints for a home or remodeling project provide the information required to determine the resources needed to successfully complete the project, estimate the cost and your anticipated profit, develop the schedule, and communicate to all parties involved what needs to be done. Blueprints provide a picture of what the finished project will look like. A business plan does all those things for your business.

Most small volume builders and remodelers never even think about writing a business plan until they are applying for a loan or seeking funding from investors. But, beyond needing to develop a plan that will impress your bank or potential investors, you want to build a solid company. You want to develop a sound strategy that will help your business grow and be successful.

But do you really need a written business plan? According to the survey of builder and remodeler members of the National Association of Home Builders (NAHB), fewer than 12 percent have a written business plan. If you were to conduct your own survey of your peers, you would probably find certain companies that have been very successful without having a written business plan and might conclude planning is a waste of time.

After all, taking the time to plan is a bit of a trade-off. Small builders and remodelers often wear multiple hats, (i.e., fill multiple roles) in the company, and each role must be filled for a business to be successful. The time you spend planning could be time spent running your company. So, why not just "get going" and learn as you build your company, instead of taking the time to formulate a plan and understand your assumptions about how your business might grow?

Here are some reasons for having a written business plan. A written plan will

- Give you greater control
- Set objectives and goals for the business and staff
- Facilitate and enhance your decision making
- Drive improved results by providing a measuring stick for performance
- Help you gain a distinctive competitive advantage
- Reveal future opportunities and concerns
- Stabilize your financial performance

- Develop team and team work that is focused on the business's future
- Allow staff to ask and answer important questions within a business
- Help you retain existing talent
- Help you attract better talent
- Improve communication
- Elevate commitment levels
- Raise motivation and morale
- Smooth out growth
- Help you anticipate and manage change
- Reduce your stress
- Help you improve your Life Balance
- Align the organization, the people, processes, and resources with a clear, captivating, and wanted future position
- If you are seeking to secure additional capital for your company, your banker will probably request a business plan

Need more reasons? Let's look at the research.

One study[3] published in 2010 titled "Should entrepreneurs plan or just storm the castle?", found that planning improved business performance.

Do you want to grow your business? Another 2010 study[1] found that plenty of businesses can find success without planning, but companies with a plan grew 30% faster, and were more successful than those that didn't plan.

Another study[2] found that the fast-growing companies—companies that had over 92% growth in sales from one year to the next—usually have business plans. In fact, 71% of fast-growing companies have plans. They create budgets, set sales goals, and document their marketing and sales strategies.

The same study[3] that found that planning improved business performance and planning benefited existing companies even more than it benefited startups.

Why would planning help a business that has a few years of history more than one that is just starting up? Because the strategies they develop are based on more information about the market, their customers, their costs, and what their needs are than a new startup does, so planning involves fewer guesses or assumptions that need to be proven.

The same study[1] that found that businesses grow faster with a plan also found that companies that did a good job defining their unique selling proposition do even better than companies who have a hard time defining their customers' needs.

Taking the simple step forward to do any planning at all will certainly put your business at a significant advantage over businesses that just drive forward with no specific plans.

Your business plan is the most important management tool you have. It defines your strategy, tactics, and specific activities for execution, including dates and deadlines, budgets and cash flow. It will guide you regarding the types of projects to pursue, how you market your company, the people to hire and the funding needed to succeed. Planning establishes your short-term and long-term goals and outlines how you can achieve those goals by breaking down long-range plans into manageable short-term goals that everyone on your team can identify and support.

Your business plan will help you focus strategy, manage milestones, manage metrics, assign and track responsibilities and performance, and manage money using projections for sales, costs, expenses, and cash.

A business plan addresses the six elements the National Association of Home Builders "Business Management for Building Professionals" course cites as necessary to the success of any business. Referred to in the course as the Six Ps, they are:

- **Purpose** – the baseline for all you hope to accomplish in the future. It defines what you want to do and what you want to achieve: your vision. It gives direction to everything you do. It communicates priorities to everyone who works with you and focuses everyone's energy and commitment on what you want the company to achieve.
- **Planning** – includes setting long-term and short-term goals, developing strategies, and outlining tasks and schedules to achieve your vision.
- **Process** – defining how you want to manage your business, choosing its legal form, developing an effective workflow, setting up systems and procedures, and gathering the resources to implement the plan so you can achieve your purpose and the goals you set.
- **People** – the human capital needed to help you run the business. Once you have outlined the company's purpose, developed your short- and long-term plan and identified the processes necessary to run your business, you can determine how many people you need.
- **Performance** – ensuring that the resources and processes you have put in place work together effectively to meet your goals. Performance includes use of effective management skills as well as tools for tracking progress. Performance is about running the business, so it doesn't run you!
- **Progress** – evaluating results to determine whether you are reaching the goals you set in your plan. It is an ongoing process, so you can adjust systems, people, or goals, as needed, as you go. What gets measured, gets changed.

Although **Perspective** is not one the six Ps, it is also an important quality for the small volume builder or remodeler to have. Perspective is the ability to see in all directions and consider all components.

Writing your business plan will give you perspective. It will give you a better understanding of the various positions within your organization and their processes and functionality. It will help you understand business cycles. It will help you recognize if and where there are problems, objectively evaluate your options and make decisions. In addition to helping you maintain appropriate focus within your company, it will help you achieve a healthy balance between work and personal life.

Whether you're developing a plan for strategic growth or to raise money for your business, a solid business plan is a key component to every successful business.

A well-written business plan is also the best way to show bankers and potential investors that you are worthy of financial support. The plan document will get you in the door and help you convince loan officers and potential investors that you can put your plan into action. It will show them that you have the tools, talent and team to make it happen.

In fact, a study at the University of Oregon[4] found businesses with a written plan were far more likely to get funding than those that didn't have a plan, which can be important to the small volume builder or remodeler seeking a line of credit or financing for a project.

So now you know *why* you need a business plan. The next chapter will provide an overview of *how* to write a business plan.

CHAPTER 3

HOW TO WRITE A BUSINESS PLAN: AN OVERVIEW

"Reduce your plan to writing. The moment you complete this, you will have definitely given concrete form to the intangible desire."

—Napoleon Hill

Most builders and remodelers aren't business experts. They're learning as they go and don't have degrees in business. Writing a business plan may seem like a difficult hurdle, but it doesn't have to be. If you know your business and are passionate about it, writing a business plan, and then leveraging your plan for growth will be easy.

While I strongly believe that every builder or remodeler should have a written business plan to help them run their business, not every builder or remodeler needs a complete, formal business plan suitable for submitting to a bank or potential investor. Your business plan should be only as big as what you need to run your business. Size your business plan to fit your building or remodeling business. Don't include outline points just because they are on a big list somewhere unless you think they will help you manage your business.

If you are seeking funding or potential investors, your business plan should be developed and presented in the standard business plan format that a banker expects to see, in the order they expect to see it in. Following a standard business plan outline will keep you on track and save you from botching your best chance at getting funded.

A formal business plan document to be read by outsiders for business purposes, such as backing a loan application or seeking investment, should follow the Detailed Business Plan Outline below:

1.0 **Executive Summary**
1.1 Company Information
1.2 Financial Performance And Forecasts
1.3 Goals
1.4 Capital Requirements
1.5 Leadership Team
1.6 Market Research And Analysis
1.7 Target Market

7.0	**Operations Plan**
7.1	Administration
7.1.1	Staffing
7.1.2	Bookkeeping And Processing Payables And Receivables
7.1.3	Job Costing
7.2	Production
7.2.1	Staffing
7.2.2	Purchasing
7.2.3	Scheduling
7.2.4	Quality Control Plan
7.2.5	Safetyinformation Technology Plan

8.0	**Leadership Team And Staffing Plan**
8.1	Leadership Team
8.2	Leadership Staffing Plan
8.3	Leadership Development Plan
8.4	Succession Plan (If Applicable)

9.0	**Goals And Action Plans**
9.1	Goals
9.2	Action Plans

10.0	**Financial Forecasts And Budgets**
10.1	Revenue Projections
10.2	Operating Expense Budget
10.3	Work In Progress Projections
10.4	Income Or Profit And Loss Statement
10.5	Balance Sheet
10.6	Cash Flow Statement
10.7	Breakeven Analysis
10.8	Pro Forma Assumptions
10.9	Key Ratios
10.10	Financial Analysis And Conclusions
10.11	Capital Requirements
10.12	Use Of Funds Statement

11.0 Review Schedule

12.0 Supporting Data Exhibits

Don't be intimidated by the detailed business plan outline. Again, your business plan should be only as big as what you need to run your business. Don't include outline points just because they are on the detailed outline unless you think it will help you manage your business or unless you're developing a standard business plan that you'll be showing to someone who expects to see a standard business plan.

Your business plan should be short and concise. The reason is twofold: 1) You want your plan to be read, and 2) you want your business plan to be accessible - something you continue to use and refine over time. An excessively long business plan is a huge hassle to deal with and guarantees your plan will be relegated to a desk drawer.

Your plan should be written in a language that your audience will understand. Keep your explanations of your product simple and direct, using terms that everyone can understand.

Use the detailed business plan outline as a checklist, and don't develop your plan in the same order as you would present the finished document.

For example, although the executive summary is the first section of the detailed business plan outline, it should be the last thing you write after you know exactly what appears in the rest of your business plan. Because it is a summary, it should be the easiest thing to write. And if you're writing an internal business plan that's purely a strategic guide for your company, you can skip the executive summary or greatly reduce it in scope.

What follows is a step-by-step guide to writing your business plan presented in the order in which I believe builders and remodelers should develop it. And I believe builders and remodelers should start with Market Research and Analysis.

CHAPTER 4

MARKET RESEARCH AND ANALYSIS

"The aim of marketing is to know and understand the customer so well the product or service fits him and sells itself."

—Peter F. Drucker

Market Research

"The housing market meltdown—and a new era of tight credit and slow growth—has radically reshaped residential home building. Where the game used to be won or lost based on instinct and speed, it's now all about crunching the right numbers." - Jonathan Smoke, Chief Economist, Hanley Wood Senior Vice President

From 1992–2006, life was good for home builders, developers, building products manufacturers and other related professionals in the U.S. Enticed by steadily rising home values and declining interest rates, builders and developers bought land and put up homes at a breathtaking rate, peaking at 1.7 million single-family housing starts in 2005.

The implosion of the housing market, followed by the worst financial meltdown since the Great Depression, has changed the playbook. In a volatile market where tight credit, skittish buyers and slow growth are the new rules of engagement, builders can no longer rely on instinct, speed and experience when making precious investments in land and housing developments.

Most small volume builders are product focused. But the key to success in the home building industry is being market-focused which equates to being customer focused.

Most small volume builder's approach to market research can be described as "follow the herd" – just do what everyone else is doing or head in the same direction as the herd – build similar homes with similar amenities in the same or similar communities. This approach to market research might work well in a strong market where the demand for new homes exceeds the supply. But in a soft market just like in nature, this approach can result in those at the back of the herd falling prey to predators – the lenders who financed those homes. And even if they are lucky enough to survive, those at the back of the herd eat a lot of dust and step in a lot of dung. So, do you really want to follow the herd?

A few small volume builders try to be pioneers. They introduce unique floor plans, styles and innovative features based, not on market research, but on their "gut feelings." But what if their "gut feelings" are wrong? You might have heard the expression "You can tell the pioneers. They're the ones with the arrows in their backs." This is the fate that awaits the pioneers who act without adequate market research.

Before the housing market imploded, such gut-level decisions— whether well or poorly made— were masked by easy credit and steadily rising real estate valuations. But in today's construction environment, those economic luxuries no longer exist. From land acquisition to pricing, home building decisions not backed by shareable, objective data are being subjected to harsh scrutiny by creditors, shareholders and other external stakeholders. This is especially true given the powerful analytic tools now available to guide a residential construction company's course. The question isn't whether these data sets will influence the market, the question is which builders will adopt them quickly enough to gain a competitive advantage.

The truth is there's opportunity at every level in the industry. According to the federal Bureau of Labor Statistics, U.S. home builders accounted for about 12 percent of all construction employment in 2008, not counting specialty trade contractors such as masons, plumbers and electricians. While there are a handful of large national builders, the industry is highly fragmented. By some estimates, there are between 150,000 to 170,000 home builders in the U.S., most of which have 50 or fewer employees. While these companies differ in size and scope, every home builder can benefit from the use of fact-based decision tools to aid profitability and growth.

The days of "build it or remodel it and they will buy" are a thing of the past. Today customers are both demanding and selective and, thanks to the world of technology, they are very well educated.

Market research is the process of learning about your potential customers. Who they are? How many of them are there? What are they buying? Where are they buying?

Market research and analysis is about identifying your "target market" – your ideal customer.

Market research provides you with the information you need to describe that customer.

Understanding your target market is key to deciding what product to build, where to build it, and how to price it. It is also key to building marketing campaigns and sales processes that work. If you don't understand your potential buyer, you don't know what kind of marketing messages and advertising will work.

Market research will greatly reduce your risk and improve your marketing and sales process. Market research doesn't have to involve tons of work.

Builders and remodelers should do four types of research.

- Demographic research
- Psychographic research
- Consumer research
- Competitive research

Demographic research and competitive research are more quantitative in nature while psycho- graphic research and consumer research are more qualitative in nature.

Demographic Research provides information on potential buyers

- Income ranges and averages
- Ages
- Genders
- Family/household structure
- Job markets
- Population/immigration trends
- Comprehensive economic /development plan, and

- Special needs populations

Psychographic Research provides information on your potential buyers

- Goals and aspirations
- Self -image
- Lifestyle
- Hobbies
- Values
- Media and communication preferences
- Buying habits

Why is this type of information useful? Understanding buyers' motivations can be difficult. Psychographics provide greater insight into the personality, values, attitudes, interests and lifestyles of your target market. Psychographic research helps ensure that:

- You are building what your buyers like (not what you like).
- Your marketing efforts effectively inform and inspire your target market.
- Your advertising fits the buyer's lifestyle and needs.

Consumer Research comes directly from your target market and provides information on their:

- Buying process
- Differentiating factor(s)

Consumer research is more current and accurate than existing research. It is more helpful to conduct consumer research after you have identified your target market. Consumer research methods and tools include focus groups, telephone surveys, model home exit surveys, website surveys, and real estate agent interviews. Consumer research is used to learn about your target market's likes and dislikes regarding:

- Product design
- Home features
- Community amenities

Focus groups are usually conducted by private consumer research companies and involve:

- Professional group leader/moderator
- Room with a one-way mirror
- Video or audio recording

Typical participants in focus groups include:

- Owners in similar communities
- Prospects
- Members of demographic or psychographic group

- Real estate agents

Telephone surveys are conducted over the phone, one-on-one, with less discussion and more closed-ended questions.

Model Home Exit Surveys are conducted as potential buyers leave models. Model home exit surveys can be either written surveys or face-to-face interviews. They ask for potential buyers' opinions on:

- The model
- The community

Website Surveys are completed on the website. They focus on the:

- Website functionality and appeal
- Product preferences of website visitors

Website surveys can also be used to gather demographic information for buyer profiles.

Real Estate agent interviews can be conducted in groups or one-on-one, either face to face or by telephone. Real estate agent interviews invite real estate agents' professional perspective on your product and their understanding of customers' needs and wants

Competitive Research provides information on your competition. It answers the question *"What types of competition exists in the market?"* Competitive research looks at new construction and resale of existing homes. For new construction, it looks at

- The Competitions' Reputations
- Market History
- Build cycles and phasing
- Traffic
- Inventory and absorption rates by price range
- New products and amenities
- Incentives and promotions
- Location

For resales, you should research

- Total number of resale homes for sale in your area
- Age of resale homes in your area
- Days on the market or absorption rate
- Pricing trends

When conducting research, you should look at all types of research and always do as much as you can in each research type.

Here are some good places to start your market research:

- **Your past and current customers:** If you have been in business for a while, your past and current customers are an invaluable resource. You can use online surveys or social media to gather feedback about buying habits, needs, and other psychographic information.
- **U.S. Census Bureau:** https://www.census.gov/ Here you'll find demographics you can use to figure out your market share. The ***Census Business Builder (CBB)*** is a suite of services that provide selected demographic and economic data from the Census Bureau tailored to specific types of users in a simple to access and use format. The **Small Business Edition** section is built primarily for small business owners who need key data for their business plan or to better understand their potential market. It presents data for a single type of business and geography at a time. Here you generate a report for your selected type of business, like Home Construction, in your geographic area – city, county, etc. You can also use the **Community Facts** section of the **American Fact Finder** to find facts on your geographic are including:
  - General Population and Housing Characteristics (Population, Age, Sex, Race, Households and Housing, ...)
  - Population Estimates
  - And Comparisons of Cities and Towns for Population, Housing, Area, and Density Search the U.S. Census website for residential construction to find information on new residential construction, building permits, characteristics of new housing, and construction spending.
- **CensusViewer:** http://censusviewer.com/free-maps-and-data-links/ This free tool gives you access to U.S. Census data in an easy-to-use format that you can explore either visually on a map or in data reports for cities, counties, and entire states.
- **Consumer Expenditure Survey:** https://www.bls.gov/cex/ The **Consumer Expenditure Surveys (CE)** program of the Bureau of Labor Statistics provides data on expenditures, income, and demographic characteristics of consumers in the United States. Data is available on a national, regional and state level and for select MSA's.
- **Zonda**: https://zondahome.com Zonda merged with Hanley Wood in 2018 an is considered the definitive authority on the residential construction real estate and housing market. Zonda maintains the nation's most comprehensive database of housing market information. Every quarter, their local field research teams deliver the most accurate market data on active and future construction in the industry. They gather deed records, tax assessors' records, and demographics, as well as economic data that provides insight into local market health the national economy. All Zonda information is accessible via their suite of cutting-edge, cloud-based applications—desktop and mobile tools that empower client teams to analyze information, run reports, and create visualizations and thematic views on client-defined maps, ranging a local neighborhood to an entire metropolitan area.
- **Claritas**: https://segmentationsolutions.nielsen.com/mybestsegments/Claritas' industry-leading consumer lifestyle segmentation provides consumer behavioral information for shopping, financial and technology preferences, media habits (online and offline) and more. These powerful consumer segmentation insights enable you to:
  - Gain detailed insights for better market planning, media strategy, and customer acquisition
  - Tailor messages and products that resonate with customers
  - Group similar segments together to maximize marketing efficiency and reach
  - Discover who your best customers are and where you can locate similar people Claritas' lifestyle segmentation systems define every household in the U.S. by distinct lifestyle types, called "segments", to provide you with a comprehensive picture of who lives where and what

they are like. MyBestSegments ZIP Code Look-up lets you view your neighborhood's household segments within any ZIP Code. Typically, a ZIP Code has over a dozen segments present, but to view your neighborhood's top five segments, along with a descriptive snapshot about each segment's characteristics for any Claritas segmentation system, simply enter your 5-digit ZIP Code. While the most detailed data is not free, you can get a lot of great insights from the free version.

- **SBDCNet Business Snapshots:** http://www.sbdcnet.org/ is the official National Information Clearinghouse of the U.S. Small Business Administration. Its **Small Business Snapshots** provides market research reports covering industry trends, market statistics, customer demographics, recent business articles, and links to industry trade associations. Its **Market Research Links** contain web resources sorted by type of industry. Search "residential construction."
- **NAHB.org**
- **Local Multiple Listing Service**
- **Local Title Companies**

A little estimation is okay, but the bulk of your numbers need to be based on facts.

Market Analysis

Once you've completed your market research, you need to analyze the information. The market analysis is one of the most important parts of your business strategy. Do it right, and you will have a clear idea of the path down which you are headed. A good market analysis will enable you to attract customers and avoid pitfalls.

If you are seeking funding, market analysis is going to be key data to convince your audience that you have the facts and hard numbers to back it up.

Market analysis is exactly what it sounds like: determining the characteristics unique to your market and analyzing this information, which will help you make decisions for your business. By conducting a market analysis, you will be able to gather valuable data that will help you get to know your customers, determine appropriate pricing, and figure out your competitors' vulnerabilities. If you do need banks to lend you money or investors to invest, a market analysis section demonstrating that your plan is viable will be required. Either way, a solid business plan complete with market analysis will be invaluable.

A market analysis can be a measuring stick you use over time to see how far you've come, and it allows you to make projections based on data rather than guesswork. Because you'll know the size of the mountain you're about to climb, you'll be able to pace yourself and prevent problems in the future.

Your market analysis should include an overview of your industry, a look at your target market, an analysis of your competition, your own projections for your business, and any regulations you'll need to comply with.

Industry and Economic Analysis

Discuss the current state of the homebuilding and remodeling industry overall and where it's headed. Relevant industry metrics like size, trends, life cycle, and projected growth should all be included here. This will let banks or investors see that you know what you're doing and have done your home- work and come prepared with the data to back up your business idea.

If your plan is for your own management purposes, you should be very sure that you know your market. If your plan is a plan to be presented to outsiders, then you need to explain the type of business you're in. You'll be expected to explain the general state of your industry and the nature of the business, especially if your plan is going outside your company to banks or investors. You want to know your industry inside and out. Read on for the kind of information you must know very well, even if you don't go to the trouble of writing it all out. And if you're writing for outsiders with a formal business plan document, then you should do an industry analysis, describing:

Everything in the residential construction and real estate industry that happens outside of your business will affect your company. The more you know about your industry, the more advantage and protection you will have.

A complete business plan discusses general industry economics, participants, distribution patterns, factors in the competition, and whatever else describes the nature of this business to outsiders.

Economic characteristics include:

- Total Employment and Employment Growth
- Employment Distribution and Growth by Industry
- Residential Building Permits
- Employment/Permit (E/P) Ratio - The E/P ratio is annual job growth in a given period divided by the number of building permits issued during that same time. This ratio uses employment growth as a gauge to show where supply is in relation to demand based on job creation. Historically, one new housing unit is required for every two new jobs.
- Current Position in the Housing Cycle
- New and Used Home Sales
- New and Used Home Inventory
- The Months' Supply of New Homes
- New Home Absorption by Builder

Market Segmentation

Market segmentation is the subdividing of consumers, customers, investors or other constituencies into homogeneous subsets or groups. These groups have some commonalities that translate to simi- larities in consumption functions or demand for products or services. Once these groups have been created, they can be targeted for a product or services by product differentiation and marketing.

There are three major types of market segmentation strategies: No Segmentation, Complete Segmentation and Concentrated Segmentation.

No Segmentation. In no segmentation, the market is offered a single product on a take it or leave it basis. The product is standard and designed to appeal to a generic class of consumer. In residential construction, this could take the form of tract housing where emphasis is on production economies rather than customer satisfaction.

Complete Segmentation. In complete segmentation, each customer is treated as an individual, with a customized solution to address their unique needs. In residential construction, this would occur in the case of custom houses. Since the emphasis is on product differentiation, there are no economies of scale which in turn, drives up unit cost per unit. The producer can select individual clients or customers, focusing on the most attractive or profitable.

Selective Segmentation. In selective segmentation, customers are grouped into clusters, with a customized solution developed for each of the targeted segments. The producer does not have to target each of the segments or groups but can concentrate on one or more. The focus can be on cap- turing some economies of scale or diversification benefits that are associated with mixes of targeted segments.

There are number of bases for segmenting real estate markets to provide a better understanding of the players for a site or asset

Geographic. This involves clustering users based on location of where they reside, work or patronize certain establishments. It is particularly useful in real estate which is fixed in location and thus inherently geographic.

Demographic. This approach uses customer characteristics to create profiles of members of various subsets. When focused on individuals, standard demographic criteria include age, income, educational attainment, ethnicity, occupation, marital status, and household size. In looking at companies, variables include size, product lines, business models, price points, and types of goods and services.

Psychographic. This approach focuses on the self-perception, aspirational hopes, or self-actualization of potential members. In a business sense, it can also refer to the branding or image of a company.

Behavioral. This approach focuses on what the customer or client does rather than who they are or what they say. It also looks at their value systems and the kinds of activity, problem-solving or decision-making processes used in making decisions regarding the selection of products or services. **Sectoral.** This refers to the line of business or employment in which potential members are involved or operate. This may be at a general level (e.g., professionals, services, medical) or at more detailed levels. I knew a builder who only built for lawyers. You need to do research to determine if your target market is big enough.

Price. This refers to the various price ranges of homes in your market.

Markets and Sub-Markets

A market is the overall set of buyers. A sub-market forms part of an overall market. The real estate market can be divided into sub-markets of neighborhoods, price, etc. Large builders and remodeler might operate in all these sub-markets, whereas small volume builders and remodelers may only operate in one or two sub-markets. This means that in each sub-market there would be a different competitive set and market structure.

Home buyers typically look for properties in a search range that depends on their geographic preferences, budget, or family size. For example, they might only consider houses in a certain price range that are also within reasonable commuting distance from their workplace. A family with chil- dren might in addition require that the house be in a good school district

As part of your company's marketing strategy, you should define the markets and/or sub-mar- kets that you choose to operate in. This is sometimes referred to as 'where to compete?' Some com- panies will map out their business scope on a product/market grid, which identifies which products they wish to offer in which markets or sub-markets.

Niche markets. We're living in the days of the niche market! You can use target marketing to carve out your own space in the marketplace. Some niche markets for builders and remodelers are the 55+ market, the sustainable building market, the high-end custom home market, and kitchen and bath remodeling

Target Market

Now that you've done your market research and analysis, it's time to define your target market.

Don't fall into the trap of defining your target market as "everyone." Your target market can be broken down into four "who, where, why and how" components:

The "WHO": Demographics

Who needs your homes or remodeling services? Include basic demographic details such as age, gender, family size, educational level, and occupation here.

The "WHERE": Geographics

Where are your customers? These are the places your customers can be found (i.e., their zip code), and be sure to learn details like the size of the area, its population density, and its climate.

The "WHY": Psychographics

Why do your customers make the choices they make? This is personality and lifestyle informa- tion that will help you figure out your customers' buying patterns. Consider what benefits you can provide over your competitors, and how loyal your customers are to you or your competitor (and why).

The "HOW": Behaviors

How do your customers behave? All customers are buying to fulfill a need, but how do they regard that need? How do they regard your product? How much information do they have on this need or how your product fulfills it, and what are their information sources?

At the bare minimum, these are the things you should know about your target customers:

- **What is their gender?** Yes, this is the 21st century, but women and men still make very different purchasing decisions for a variety of complex reasons.
- **How old are they?** "18-49" won't fly anymore. Millennials? GenX? Boomers? The Silent Generation?
- **What are their interests or hobbies?** Finding out what people are into will help you connect with them.
- **Where do they currently live?** Statistical data show that 64% of Americans who move each year move within the same county.
- **How long have they lived there?** Statistical data show that the average American moves once every 5 years.
- **How do they make a living?**
- **How much money do they make?**
- **Do they own their own homes, or do they rent?**

What strikes you as an untapped opportunity? Did you hear the same or similar complaints/ sugges- tions from multiple people?

Target marketing is a tool you can employ if you are looking for an opportunity to grow your business or want to protect the business you've already built.

Use the attributes you defined in this step to figure out how many people meet your demo- graphic, psychographic, or location criteria. How big is your target market? What is its growth rate? What is the general outlook and trends for this market. Who are your main competitors?

This process is critical because it might help you re-define your target market. Your initial assumptions regarding your target market might be wrong. That's OK. If there aren't enough potential customers to sustain your business and your competitors, then you need to change your target market. Better to make mistakes early in the planning process before you've risked very much.

It's important to establish a clear idea of your target market. By narrowing in on your real customers, you'll be able to direct your marketing dollars efficiently while attracting loyal customers who will spread the word about your business. You do need to know who your customer is and have a rough estimate of how many of them there are. If there aren't enough customers for your product or service, that could be a warning sign.

Identify your market segments to determine how big each segment is. A market segment is a group of people that you could potentially sell to.

A good business plan will identify the target market segments and then provide some data to indicate how fast each segment is growing.

Once you have identified your key market segments, you should discuss the trends for these markets. Are they growing or shrinking? Discuss the market's evolving needs, tastes, or other upcoming changes to the market.

Once you have your target market segments defined, it's time to define your ideal customer for each segment. Your ideal customer is a fictitious representation of your market and is often called a "buyer persona" or "user persona." A persona is a description of a person that hits on all the key aspects of your target market. Your buyer persona should be defined with a name, gender, income level, likes, dislikes, etc. While this may seem like additional work on top of the market segmentation that you have already done, having a solid buyer persona will be an extremely useful tool to help you define the kinds of marketing and sales activities you will develop to attract these ideal customers. The single piece of documentation that every business should create is a buyer persona. And, just like you might have several target markets for your business, you might have several different buyer personas.

Creating a buyer persona converts your target marketing information from dry research into a living, breathing person.

- **User persona and characteristics:** You'll want to include demographics such as age, income, and location here. You'll also need to dial into your customers' psychographics as well. You should know what their interests and buying habits are, as well as be able to explain why you're in the best position to meet their needs.
- **Market size:** This is where you want to get real, both with yourself and the potential readers of your business plan. Do your research and find out who and where your competitors are. How big is the potential market for your business?

Main Competitors

Once you have identified your target market, you need to figure out if your target market is big enough to sustain your business. It is essential to understand the nature of competition in your market. This is still in the general area of describing the industry.

This is the section in which you dissect your competitors. You need to know what you're up against. Explain the general nature of competition in the building and remodeling business.

How are buyers or homeowners selecting one builder or remodeler over another. What buying factors make the most difference—is it Product? Price? Product? Place? Service? What are the keys to success?

You need to look for the competition's weaknesses. Are there customers that are being under- served? What can you offer that other builders and remodelers aren't offering? The competitive analysis should contain the following components.

Do a very complete analysis of your main competitors. Make a list of your top 5 or 10 competitors. List each one separately and do a Comparative Analysis. Know everything about your competition. Conduct a market analysis to learn what they're doing. Are they serving a market gap — an unmet demand? If they are offering the same thing, is there enough market share to go around? What must you do to gain market share? It is essential to decide if and how to compete with them, especially on pricing.

What are the strengths and weaknesses of each? Consider their products, pricing, reputation, management, financial position, brand awareness, business development, or other factors that you feel are important. In what segments of the market do they operate? What seems to be their strategy? How much do they impact your products, and what threats and opportunities do they represent?

What is your competition good at? Where do they fall behind? Get imaginative to spot opportunities to excel where others are falling short. Conduct a Comparative Analysis:

- Compare your portfolio of plans to the competitions.
- Compare home features.
- Compare base pricing.
- Determine the adjusted sales price of the competition's homes.
  - For features only you offer, subtract value to the competition's price.
  - For features only the competition offers, add value from the competition's price.
  - Use your pricing.

Describe each of your major competitors in terms of those same factors. Your description might also include their size, the market share they command, their comparative product quality, their growth, available capital and resources, image, marketing strategy, target markets, or whatever else you consider important.

Specifically describe the strengths and weaknesses of each competitor and compare them to your own. Consider their service, pricing, reputation, management, financial position, brand awareness, business development, or other factors that you feel are important. In what segments of the market do they operate? What seems to be their strategy? How much will they impact your business, and what threats and opportunities do they represent?

Comparing your product with your competitors will help you determine how you should price your products or services, what the most critical features or benefits are, and what features your customers want.

The importance of your target market to competitors: Ideally, you're going after customers whose needs aren't being met by your competitors.

Finding Information on Competitors

You can find an amazing wealth of market data on the Internet. The hard part, of course, is sorting through it and knowing what to stress.

Your access to competitive information will vary, depending on where you are and who the competition is. If possible, you may want to take on the task of playing the role of a potential customer and gain information from that perspective.

Industry associations, industry publications, media coverage, information from the financial community, and their own marketing materials and websites may be good resources to identify these factors and "rate" the performance and position of each competitor.

Barriers to Entry

What are the potential pitfalls of entering your market? What's the cost of entry? This is where you examine *your* weaknesses. Be honest, with investors and yourself. Being unrealistic is not going to make you look good.

Window of Opportunity

Do you need to get in early to take advantage of an emerging market?

In other words, you should know how you are positioned in the market. Why do people buy your product or services instead of the others offered in the same general categories? What benefits do you offer at what price, to whom, and how does your mix compare to others? Think about specific kinds of benefits, features, and market groups, comparing where you think you can show the difference.

Business Risks

What are the potential business risks facing your company and how will you deal with them. Common risks might include:

- **Competition:** How will you monitor the competition?
- **Industry growth rate:** How will you monitor the industry growth rate in your market, in those markets whose in-migration contributes to your target market, and nationally.
- **Demand:** How will you monitor demand?
- **Labor availability:**
- **Cost and profitability:**
- **Profit erosion:**
- **Professional liability:**
- **Economic risks:** Consider things like interest rates, projected employment growth.
- **Weather:**
- **Regulations:** Are there any specific governmental regulations or restrictions on your market? If so, you'll need to bring them up here and discuss how you're going to comply with them. You will

also need to address the cost of compliance. Addressing these issues is essential if you are seeking investment or money from a lender, and everything must be legally squared away and above board.

Completing your market research and analysis early will help you refine your business model and make a clear impact on your future success. You need to identify your potential customers, and it will help you to be clear about what you want to do with your business, both now and in the future. The time you spend doing the research and putting it all together will come back to you many times over in dollars earned and heartbreaks avoided. You'll look like a professional, and you'll outshine the competitors that didn't write one.

Now that you have defined your target market, your next step is to develop your Product and Service Plan.

CHAPTER 5

PRODUCT AND SERVICE PLAN

"Don't find customers for your products, find products for your customers."

—Seth Godin

The Products and Services Plan section of your business plan is where you describe in detail the problem that you're solving, your solution, and how your product and service fit into the existing competitive landscape. Use this section of your business plan to demonstrate what sets your solution apart from others, and how you plan to expand your offerings in the future.

The Four "P" s of marketing are Product, Place, Price, and Promotion. Your product and ser- vice strategy will address the first three – Product, Place, and Price – as well as service. Promotion will be covered in the Market and Sales Plan.

A complete business plan describes what you sell: not only the homes you build or the remodeling projects you specialize in, but also the customer service you provide. This part of the plan is mainly description. In a standard business plan, it normally appears after the company description, but before the market analysis. However, I believe builders and remodelers need to do their market analysis and define their target market before deciding what to build or what projects to specialize in, where to build or remodel, and what to charge.

If you are an existing company, this section may detail key factors about the products that you are building now and plan on building in the future.

Product

Describe the type of product(s) you build or plan to build, i.e. entry-level, move-up, custom, multi-family, etc., or the type of remodeling projects you specialize in, i.e. whole house remodels, kitchen and bath remodels, remodeling for aging-in-place, etc.

Place

Describe the communities in which your company builds or plans on building, or in which your remodeling business operates, and why you chose those locations.

Price

Most builders and remodelers simply use a multiplier to determine the price. They multiply their cost by a multiplier like 1.15 or 1.20 without any consideration as to whether that multiplier pro- duces an accurate market value or provides an adequate reward for the risk they are assuming for each individual project. As Ken Brookings of the Aspire Institute notes in his program "Where Does Profit Really Come From?", this method of determining the sales price by "marking up" the cost by a certain percentage is one small math step and not a business strategy or a price driver.

Instead of simply using a standard multiplier to markup the cost, you should determine the price based on a "gross margin" strategy. While markup is the amount by which the cost of a product is increased to derive the selling price, margin (also known as gross margin) is the sales price minus the cost of goods sold. A gross margin strategy takes into consideration your projected revenue, financing costs, sales and marketing expenses, general and administrative expenses, your products and services, your competition, where you want to be positioned in your market, i.e. at the high-end or low-end, how many projects you will have going at one time, how long it will take to complete the house or remodeling project, and your desired net profit.

Another pricing strategy is "value-based pricing." Value-based pricing is a pricing strategy which sets prices primarily, but not exclusively, according to the perceived value of a product or service to the customer, rather than according to the cost of the product. Customers place value based on the product's theoretical ability to fulfill a need and provide satisfaction - also referred to as utility.

Consumer utility refers to the amount of satisfaction a product provides and how it relates to demand. Products with higher utility within their market sector can achieve higher prices than competitors perceived to have less utility. Higher utility can also equate to higher demand within the consumer market. Based on the supply and demand model, products that are higher in demand can often charge higher prices in comparison to competitors with lower demand.

Brand names can alter perceived value. Products, such as plumbing fixtures and appliances, have similar production costs from one brand to another, yet consumers are often willing to pay more for certain brands.

Do your products offer features and benefits that fulfill a need and provide satisfaction for your target market that aren't offered by your competitors, like a tub and shower in the Master Bath, a walk-in shower, custom closet packages, a three car or four car garage, recognized brand name plumbing fixtures and appliances, or sustainable construction?

Service

There are essentially two ways builders and remodelers can differentiate themselves in the market – Product or Process. The problem with trying to differentiate yourself by product is that it's easy for your competitors to copy. If you have a good or unique product located in a desirable neighborhood and priced competitively, other builders and remodelers are eventually going to copy it. Remember the "follow the herd" approach to market research I referred to in the previous chapter? Process is much harder to emulate and therefore less likely to be copied.

For the builder and remodeler, process refers to your approach to customer service: the level and quality of service you provide your customers. Customer service is about how your keep your clients happy during and after the sale: how you manage every phase of customer interaction from the initial contact through construction, the warranty period, and beyond.

Positioning

Your Product and Pricing Strategy should focus on how you want to position your company and your product(s) and service(s) in your market. Positioning is where your company sits within the competitive landscape. How are your competitors positioning themselves?

When describing your product(s) and service(s), you need to describe the specific problem or problems your product(s) and service(s) solve for your target market. What are your customers' primary needs and wants? What solutions, if any, are currently available in their submarket? Describe the choices a potential buyer has in the market. Consider product mix, features and benefits, and price, and describe how your product compares with the specific competitors you identified in the market research and analysis section. Describe how your product addresses specific weaknesses in your competitors' products. Describe how your product compares to their product strengths.

Describe the important competitive features of your product. What features, and benefits do you offer that your competitors don't? Do you offer more square footage for the price; a wider variety of floor plans; customizable plans; more options regarding selections; more features and bene- fits; higher quality, more well-known brands; a better warranty; or a professional designation like NAHB's Certified Graduate Builder or Certified Graduate Remodeler?

Describe your customer service strategy and your project planning process. How do you work with your customers to understand their expectations and ensure that their expectations sync with your product quality standards and service criteria? How do you communicate with your customers? Do you have regularly scheduled meetings? Do your methods of communication sync with your customers preferred methods? What type of warranty do you provide and how do you administer it. A good customer service strategy will enhance your repeat and referral sales

Future Products and Services:

Finally, you want to discuss your plans for future products or services – your long-term product strategy. Did your market research uncover any emerging sub-markets that offer opportunities for growth, like the +55 market? What do the local municipalities growth plans tell you about emerging geographic areas for growth. Include a paragraph or two about potential future plans but avoid let- ting your plan become dominated by long-range plans that may or may not come to fruition.

Now that you have defined your target market and your products and services, the next step is to develop your marketing and sales plan.

CHAPTER 6

MARKETING AND SALES PLAN

"Nothing happens until someone sells something."

– Thomas J. Watson

The National Association of Home Builders' "Business Management for Building Professionals" course identifies the three functional areas of a company as

- Sales
- Administration
- Production

The roles in the Sales function are:

- Marketing Manager
- Social media Director
- Public Relations Director
- Sales Representative / Manager
- Designer
- Estimator

The Marketing and Sales Plan section of your business plan describes the Sales Function and details the strategies that you will use to promote your products and services to your target market. It also describes your sales processes and provides a blueprint for your company to communicate with potential buyers to generate leads and to close sales.

One of the common reasons given for business failure is the absence of a workable marketing plan. You might wonder how that can be with all the books, software, and free information on the Internet about creating marketing plans. Whatever the reasons, too many companies lack the right plans to take them where they want to go. This chapter will help you develop a workable plan.

Marketing Plan

In the Product and Pricing Plan chapter, you addressed the first three of the Four "P" s of marketing: Product, Place, and Price. The Marketing Plan addresses the fourth "P": Promotion.

Branding

Promotion begins with branding. Branding is an essential element of your Marketing Plan. Branding involves producing the right image of your company and products. You are your own unique brand. Your brand is the customer's perception of you versus his perception of your competition. Branding helps you stand out from your competition and is reflected in every aspect of your business:

- The messages you deliver through your website, proposals, and campaigns
- The images you convey (including of yourself)
- The way your employees interact with customers

The goal of branding is to differentiate you from your competitors and encourage prospects to select you and buy your products and services. Your brand needs to clearly communicate what makes your product and/or service special. When creating your brand, it is important to be consistent and to use professional photography. Another effective element of branding is to solicit testimonials (in writing or via video) from past customers and industry professionals who are familiar with you and your products and services.

Graphic Design

Graphic design is an important element in promotion. Graphic design is involved in creating your company logo, your website, your social media pages, your collateral material, yard signs, billboards, vehicle signage, direct mail, and specialty publications. Effective graphic design should be unique; professional; clean, clear, crisp and concise; and tailored for your target market. To insure your graphic design, is effective, make sure your logo reflects what the company does and that it fits on signage. Make sure your graphics resonate with the rest of your content. Don't use clip art or gal- lery art. Remember, less is more. Use a lot of white space in ads. And use high quality imagery and photography.

Promotion

The primary purpose of promotion is lead generation. Your Marketing Plan details your lead generation strategy - how you plan on communicating with your prospects and customers to generate leads and traffic. Your lead generation strategy should consist of the following:

- Inbound Marketing
- Outbound Marketing
- Realtors
- Public Relations

- Referrals

Inbound Marketing

Inbound marketing for builders, remodelers, and trade contractors is primarily web-based, and positions the company to be easily found on the Internet, drawing customers in as they search. Inbound marketing provides information, an improved customer experience, and builds trust by offering potential customers information they value via company sponsored newsletters, blogs and entries on social media platforms.

Marketing strategist David Meerman Scott says that inbound marketing allows marketers to "earn their way" into a customer's awareness rather than invading their awareness through paid advertisements.

The term "inbound marketing" was coined by HubSpot CEO, Brian Halligan and is synonymous with the concept of Permission Marketing a 1999, book by Seth Godin. [1][2]

> *"Inbound marketing focuses on creating quality content that pulls people toward your company and product, where they naturally want to be. By aligning the content you publish with your customer's interests, you naturally attract inbound traffic that you can then convert, close, and delight over time."*
>
> —Brian Halligan

Inbound marketing is permission-based marketing. There are two premises here:

- First, communicate via mediums in which the audience has given you permission to communicate.
- Second, answer the questions people are asking and proliferate those answers around the web in anticipation of the question.

Inbound marketing includes your website, search engine optimization (SEO), social media marketing, e-newsletters, videos, blogs, podcasts, and content marketing like eBooks and whitepapers, which serve to attract customers through the different stages of the purchase funnel.

Statistics leave no doubt that your internet marketing efforts are crucial to the success of your business. Here are just a few from the National Association of Realtors (NAR) 2012 Profile of Home Buyers and Sellers:

- 100% of home shoppers used the internet to research a specific home
- 90% of home buyers searched online at some point during their home buying process
- 86% of recent buyers said online websites were the most useful
- 44% of recent buyers said the first step that they took in the home buying process was to look online at properties for sale
- 52% of first-time buyers started their search online
- 47% of first-time home buyers used the Internet to search for a home
- 73% of senior home buyers go online to search for a home
- 39% of senior home buyers began their research online
- 30% of senior home buyers first learned about the home they eventually purchase online
- Home builder related searches on tablets grew 362% year-over-year

And the NAR 2013 Profile of Home Buyers and Sellers revealed that

- 42% of home buyers said their first step in the home-buying process was looking online
- 14% of home buyers first looked online for information about the home buying process

Website

Your website is the foundation of your web-based inbound marketing strategy. Your website is a showcase for your products or services. When designing your website, use good photography. Among buyers who used the internet during their home search, more than 85% of buyers found photos and detailed information about properties for sale very useful.

Consider what is the one feature of your company that you want clients to notice immediately. If your consumers could only stay on your site for 10 seconds, what would be the one thing they would leave knowing? Do you want to include a blog page or members-only forum?

Think about other websites you've visited. Are there any websites that you hate? Are there any that you love? Can you pinpoint one or two things about those sites that make you love or hate them?

Buyers using online resources during their home search are accessing them from a variety of devices, most often desktop computers (77%), followed by mobile devices (56%) and mobile apps (48%). Mobile applications were used by 68% of new home shoppers at the onset and throughout their research. 51% of new home shoppers read general home information on mobile devices and 89% of new home shoppers use a mobile search engine at the onset and throughout their research. Utilizing mobile devices to search for homes is most prevalent among buyers under age 50, with 66% of Millennial buyers and 62% of Generation X buyers accessing via mobile, compared to 42% of Baby Boomers and just 20% of the Silent Generation.

Use responsive web design (RWD.) According to Wikipedia contributors, "Responsive web design (RWD) is an approach to web design aimed at crafting sites to provide an optimal viewing experience — easy reading and navigation with a minimum of resizing, panning and scrolling — across a wide range of devices (from desktop computer monitors to mobile phones)." It means that the site can adapt to any size screen for better and easier user experience.

Once you've created your website, ensure your website is current and relevant in your marketplace. Ideally, update your website every two years and update your social media profile every six months. Make sure your website is mobile friendly – that it functions and displays effectively on all devices. Google's search algorithms now put a significant weight on the "mobile friendliness" of sites. Make sure your website is search engine optimized. Search engine optimization (SEO) refers to "the process of affecting the visibility of a website or a web page in a search engine's 'natural' or un-paid ('organic') search results." (Wikipedia contributors, 2014)

Social Media

Social media should be another element of your web-based inbound marketing strategy. Social media marketing (SMM) takes advantage of social networking to help a company increase brand exposure and broaden customer reach. The goal is to create content compelling enough that users will share it with their social networks. These days, having a social media presence is essentially a requirement for builders and remodeler. More and more, prospects are using social media to learn about companies and to find out how responsive they are. Social media channels include:

- **Facebook** - A popular free social networking website that allows registered users to create profiles, upload photos and video, send messages and keep in touch with friends, family and colleagues. According to the PEW Research Center, in 2016 roughly eight-in-ten online Americans (79%) use Facebook. Young adults continue to report using Facebook at high rates, but older adults are joining in increasing numbers. Some 62% of online adults ages 65 and older now use Facebook. In addition, women continue to use Facebook at somewhat higher rates than men: 83% of female internet users and 75% of male internet users are Facebook adopters.
- **Twitter** - A free microblogging service that allows registered members to broadcast short posts called tweets. Twitter members can broadcast tweets and follow other users' tweets by using multiple platforms and devices. According to the PEW Research Center, in 2016, 21% of all U.S. adults use Twitter. Roughly one-quarter of online adults (24%) use Twitter. Younger Americans are more likely than older Americans to be on Twitter. Some 36% of online adults ages 18-29 are on the social network. Among online adults ages 65 and older, just 10% of whom are Twitter users. Twitter is also somewhat more popular among the highly educated: 29% of internet users with college degrees use Twitter, compared with 20% of those with high school degrees or less.
- **Google+** - Pronounced Google plus is Google's social networking project, designed to rep- licate the way people interact offline more closely than is the case in other social network- ing services. The project's slogan is "Real-life sharing rethought for the web." Google+ has 375 million active members, 55% of them in the United States, and receives 27 million of unique monthly visits. 22% of online adults visit Google+ at least once a month. 30% of smartphone users that use the Google+ app at least once a month. 28% people age 15-34 that use Google+. 26.3% of Google+ users are female. 73.7% are male. 70% of brands that have a presence on Google+.
- **LinkedIn** - A social networking site designed specifically for the business community. The goal of the site is to allow registered members to establish and document networks of people they know and trust professionally. According to the PEW Research Center, in 2016, 29% of online adults report using the site. Half (50%) of online adults with college degrees are on LinkedIn, compared with 27% of those who have attended but not graduated from college and just 12% of those with high school degrees or less. Similarly, 45% of online adults with an annual household income of $75,000 or more use LinkedIn, compared with just 21% of those living in households with an annual income of less than $30,000. And 35% of online adults who are employed use LinkedIn, compared with 17% of those who are not employed for pay.
- **Houzz** - A website and online community about architecture, interior design and deco- rating, landscape design and home improvement. The Houzz platform and mobile apps feature photos, articles, product recommendations, and a user forum. Houzz has 35 mil- lion users. 72% of Houzz users are between the ages of 25 and 52. 90% of Houzz users are homeowners.
- **Pinterest** - A social curation website for sharing and categorizing images found online. Pinterest requires brief descriptions, but the focus of the site is visual. Clicking on an image will take you to the original source. According to the PEW Research Center, in 2016, roughly three-in-ten online Americans (31%) use Pinterest. Women use Pinterest at much higher rates than men. Nearly half of online women use the virtual pinboard (45%), more than double the share of online men (17%) who do so.
- **Instagram** - A mobile photo-sharing application and service that allows users to share pictures and videos either publicly or privately, as well as through a variety of other social networking platforms, such as Facebook, Twitter, Tumblr, and Flickr. According to the PEW Research Center, in 2016, around one-third of online adults (32%) report using Instagram. Instagram use is especially high

among younger adults. Roughly six-in-ten online adults ages 18-29 (59%) use Instagram, nearly double the share among 30- to 49-year-olds (33%) and more than seven times the share among those 65 and older (8%). Female internet users are more likely to use Instagram than men (38% vs. 26%).

- **YouTube** – A large scale video sharing site. According to its 2011 Google & Complete Home Shopper Survey, YouTube accounts for 51% of online video home research usage. According to comScore data, YouTube reaches 81.2% of Internet users in the United States. 31.8 million users aged 18 to 24 in the United States accessed YouTube at least once in the past month, accounting for 98% of internet users in that age demographic.

  YouTube attracted 19.4 million visitors 65 and older to the site in the last month, which is 3 out of 4 internet users in this age demographic. The 65+ age demographic spends 3 hours and 54 minutes on YouTube each month. People in the 55+ age demo- graphic make up 18% of the YouTube audience. 21% of YouTube users say that they visit the site daily, 28% say the check it out at least a few times per week, and 10% of people in all demographics say that they visit YouTube once per week. Men make up 55% of views on YouTube, women 45%. 86% of home shoppers find out more information about a specific community through online videos. 70% of home shoppers toured the inside of a home through online videos.

Video

Video can help you provide improved user engagement, create brand awareness, and increase SEO. Videos are a very effective way to present tours of homes and projects, product descriptions (e.g., types of insulation or carpeting), design trends, a look behind the scenes, share testimonials, and introduce yourself and your business you — as an expert, as the go-to solution in a specific geo- graphic area, and testimonials. However, it is important that they look professional. It is also important that you ensure they can be accessed on all devices and that the video and audio, if included, are of good quality. Your videos should also incorporate action. Tell a story. Do not create a video that consists only of a talking head. Whenever possible, show customers in the video. Make sure your video meets Occupational Safety & Health Administration (OSHA) requirements.

You don't need to be on every social media channel, but you do need to be on the ones that your potential customers are on. When selecting social media channels, consider the demographic for your target market. How old are they? According to the 2015 NAR Home Buyer and Seller Generational Trends Report, the frequency of internet use in the home search process was directly related to age. Younger buyers are not only more likely to use the internet during their search, but they also use the internet more frequently during their home search process. Older buyers are more likely than younger buyers to be more occasional users during their home search.

When using social media marketing (SMM) to market your business, be sure to share what makes sense for your business. Do your research, know your audience, and track your sources. Have a conversation with your audience; never be rude. Mistakes happen. Acknowledge complaints, be sincere and make it right. Do not engage in bad mouthing your competition.

Make SEO and SMM work together by incorporating your keywords in all your content. Focus your efforts. Create a game plan and stick to it.

E-newsletters

Another element of your web-based inbound marketing strategy you might consider is e-newsletters. E-newsletters are communications distributed electronically, usually on a regular basis or trig- gered by events. Types of e-newsletters used for marketing purposes include monthly, bimonthly or quarterly newsletters; welcome emails (i.e., automated responses to new subscribers when they join your email list); educational information (to help solve a subscriber's problem or answer questions); birthday and holiday greetings; event announcements (e.g., for webinars, presentations and confer- ences); anniversary messages (i.e., triggered by the anniversary that a subscriber joined your email list); re-engagement emails (to maintain a clean email list by identifying and keeping only those subscribers who are truly interested in hearing from you); and emails triggered by website affinity (i.e., emails with content relevant to the interests subscribers indicate when visiting your website);

You can use fee-based e-newsletter service providers such as Constant Contact (www.constant- contact.com), MailChimp (www.mailchimp.com), and iContact (www.icontact.com).

If you decide to us e-newsletters, you should consider what frequency is most appropriate. If it isn't meaningful to the subscriber, don't send it. For example, remodeling clients don't remodel every month. Good content is more important than high frequency.

You will also have to decide how you will obtain email addresses. Will you ask your clients for them or use a lead generation service?

Blog Blogging is another element of your web-based inbound marketing strategy which you might consider. Webster's defines a blog as *"a journal or diary written for public viewing on a website and consisting typically of personal reflections, commentary on current events, etc. arranged chronologically."* You can use your blog to answer questions for your readers. This keeps readers interested and gives them a reason to finish the blog as well as explore past postings. Whenever possible, include distinct visuals and images to enhance your message. They are attention grabbing and prepare the reader for what lies ahead. Include social media icons to make it easy for readers to stay connected with regular updates across various platforms. If you include a blog as part of your inbound market- ing strategy, be sure to keep it up to date and post on a regular basis – 3 to 5 times a week

Your blog could be a page on your website or you could use one of free blogging sites like Eblogger, Tumblr, WordPress, Quora, or Google+.

Content Marketing

Another web-based inbound marketing strategy is engaging in what is called content marketing. It's when you publish useful information, tips, and advice—usually made available for free—so that your target market can get to know your company through the expertise that you deliver. Content marketing is about teaching and educating your prospects on topics that they are interested in, not just on the features and benefits that you offer. Content marketing includes eBooks and white papers.

Pay-to-Play

Finally, your web-based inbound marketing strategies might include "Pay-to-Play" leads. You can use pay-per-click advertising on search engine sites like Google, Bing, and Yahoo. The following website will also generate leads for you:

- Contractors for hire
- Angie's List (www.angieslist.com)
- Callbox (www.callboxinc.com)
- HomeAdvisor (www.homeadvisor.com)
- Idea2Result (www.idea2result.com)

Non-web-based inbound marketing strategies would include model homes, Parade of Homes, and trade shows.

Outbound Marketing

Outbound marketing is the opposite of inbound marketing, where the customers find you. Outbound marketing tries to reach consumers through general media advertising as well as through in-person contact. Depending on the venue, the approach can be extremely broad (TV advertising), thoroughly personal (face-to-face meetings), or "impersonally personal" (cold-calling or blanket emails.) Through each outbound method, sales leads are generated and then followed by internal sales representatives.

As the Internet and mobile devices grow in popularity and offer new and creative methods of advertising, outbound marketing has lost some of its longstanding appeal.

Outbound Marketing consists of:

- TV/radio advertisements.
- Telemarketing/cold-calling.
- Newspaper advertising.
- Direct mail (brochures, postcards, catalogues)
- Email marketing
- Collateral material

As part of your outbound marketing strategy, you could take advantage of co-op advertising opportunities for TV and radio advertisements, newspaper advertising, and direct mail. For builders, remodelers, and trade contractors, co-op advertising would involve partnering with other companies whose products you specify and use in your projects, such as windows, plumbing fixtures, HVAC equipment, etc. to share the cost of advertising.

Collateral material includes brochures and flyers. If you hold a professional designation for the National Association of Home Builders, this could include brochures promoting the advantages to your customers of selecting you.

Realtors

For small volume builders and remodelers, cultivating working relationships with realtors can be a valuable lead generation strategy. Customers working with realtors are significantly more likely to purchase than those who are out alone. Just as you conducted market research to identify your target market and create your buyer persona, your strategy for cultivating mutually beneficial working relationships with realtors should include identifying and connecting with Realtors you would prefer to work with. Your strategy could include developing and implementing a coopportunity program to encourage Realtors to bring you clients. It could include making presentations at office sales meetings. It could include utilizing Association of Realtors forms and agreements to increase realtors "comfort level" when bringing you clients.

Your strategy could include connecting with realtors on social media sites like Facebook and LinkedIn.

Your strategy could also include sponsoring or participating in local Realtor association pro- grams and events. It could also include participating in your local HBA's Sales and Marketing Council, if your local association has one.

Your strategy could also include teaching education courses for Realtors.

Public Relations

Public relations is another lead generation strategy. Public relations activities build your image and enhance your identity. Public relations activities include sponsoring community and charitable events; networking with leaders in your community, local reporters and editors; volunteering to give speeches, seminars or presentations; sending a company newsletter (or e-newsletter) to previous customers, prospects, the real estate community, residents in rental communities in the area, newspaper editors and radio station news editors; obtaining testimonials from satisfied customers and featuring them in your marketing media or even displaying them in your office.

Public relations activities can also include arranging for the distribution digitally or on radio or television of advertorials (i.e., favorable stories in the media, written by you or your ad agency, appearing like news and reading as an editorial); hard news publicity stories about grand openings, award recognitions or association installations; feature stories (i.e., interviews that describe you and your company and reasons for your success; and regular press releases for all newsworthy event such as a new model opening, new floor plans in your inventory, a new phase of home sites, new employees, grand opening announcements and interesting information gathered through your market research.

Getting the media to cover you can be a great way to reach your customers. Getting a prominent review of your product or service can give you the exposure you need to grow your business.

Referrals

Your lead generation strategy should include referrals. Your referral strategy will focus on using your existing customer base to generate leads. Using referrals from existing customers can put your marketing program into overdrive, as this key group is a fresh source of satisfied customers with access to an untapped reserve of new ones. The benefits of focusing on new customer lead generation from referrals are:

- It costs less – Developing a relationship with a cold lead takes longer and costs more than it will to nurture a referral. You'll spend more time on the phone or pay more for ads to get a cold lead, because that lead has no connection with your business. A referral, on the other hand, has an existing connection with your business, generally in the form of positive word-of-mouth testimonials from friends or family.
- It'll net you the right kind of customers – Identifying satisfied customers from which to source referrals nets you more satisfied customers. This self-perpetuating cycle of highly satisfied customers boosts your ROI in multiple ways.
- It will increase revenue – Experts estimate that a lead gained from a referral will close at a rate as high as 60 percent, whereas a cold lead, or non-qualified lead will close at a rate as low as 10 percent. It pays to focus on qualified, referred leads.

Statistically, 58% of Millennials, 52% of Generation X buyers, 42% percent of Baby Boomers, and 37% of the Silent Generation turn to a relative, friend, or neighbor for information and recommendations during their home search.

To have a successful referral program, you need to keep your customers happy. Happy customers refer their friends and colleagues. Sometimes you won't even have to ask. Your best customers might also turn out to be your hardest-working "unpaid" marketing staff.

Your referral program might include rewarding the people who refer you to prospective leads. If your referral program includes rewarding your customers who participate in your lead generation referral program, you will need to consider the value of a sales lead. Examine your conversion rates and calculate the value of a customer. Is it worth it to your company to offer $100 or more for each new sales lead? You need to make sure your investments are profitable.

When developing your lead generation strategy, you need to consider your target market's characteristics and preferences. If you select your methods based on that information, you are more likely to make sound decisions about the promotional tactics that, when targeted appropriately, will generate prospects and open the door to increased sales.

Describe the lead generation strategies you plan to use and why you chose them.

If you are creating a formal business plan document to be read by outsiders for business purposes such as backing a loan application or seeking investment following the Detailed Business Plan Outline, you should include specific pieces of sales literature and collateral material in the appendices to your Business Plan. When a plan is presented to someone outside the company, sales literature is a practical way to both explain your services and present the look and feel of the company.

Sales Plan

In the Marketing Plan portion of your Marketing and Sales Plan, you described your lead generation strategy. The Sales Plan portion of your Marketing and Sales Plan details your plan for converting the leads generated by your marketing into clients.

Qualifying Leads

The first step in converting leads in clients is to qualify those leads. You need to determine the leads potential for turning into a sale. Qualifying your leads involves finding out the answers to a number of questions.

What lead generation strategy brought you the lead? Was it inbound marketing, outbound marketing, a realtor, a referral, or is the lead a repeat customer? If it was inbound marketing, which inbound marketing element generated the lead? Was it your website, one of your social media sites, and if so, which one specifically, your e-newsletter, your blog, your content marketing, or pay-to- play advertising? If it was outbound marketing, which outbound marketing element generated the lead? Was it your TV or radio ad, a cold-call, your newspaper ad, your direct mail campaign, your email marketing, or your content marketing? Was the lead generated by a realtor or a referral?

How serious is the lead? Where are they in the process of purchasing? Are they just gathering information or are they ready to make a commitment? What is their budget and is it realistic? How do they intend to finance their project? If they are a homebuyer, have they pre-qualified with a lender? If they are potential remodeling clients, have they tried to do the work themselves and, if so, what were their results? What is their time frame and is it realistic?

Describe your plan for qualifying leads.

Tracking Leads

Another key component of your Sales Plan is developing a system for tracking and analyzing leads. Tracking and analyzing leads is important because it provides you with reliable data you can analyze to determine how well your lead generation strategies are working. Your lead tracking system should track the source and quality of the lead. Your lead qualification system will provide this data.

Your lead tracking system should track the cost of leads. What was the cost per lead? To determine the cost per lead, divide the total amount spent on the lead generation strategy that produced the lead by the total number of leads generated.

Your system should also track the result of leads. Did the lead turn into an appointment? Was the lead eventually converted into a sale? What was the cost of the converted lead – the cost per sale? To determine the cost per sale, divide the total amount spent on the lead generation strategy that produced the lead by the total number of sales which resulted.

How profitable was the project?

Lead tracking and analyzing is important because it allows you to determine which lead generation strategies are generating the highest quality leads come, which strategies brought you leads that converted into sales, and which strategies brought you the most profitable work.

Describe your lead tracking system.

Estimating

Because estimating is a role of the Sales function, the Sales Plan portion of your Marketing and Sales Plan should describe your estimating procedure.

Regardless of whether your product is spec homes, custom homes, or remodeling projects, it is important to have a Standard Estimating Procedure (SEP) that can be replicated time after time to provide a consistent result. An effective estimating system enables you to determine costs, set the selling price, control costs and evaluate whether the project is a fit for you. The most important factors for a successful estimating system are accuracy, speed and clarity.

The estimating process is a key component of every home building and remodeling company because each project that the company undertakes depends on an accurate analysis or estimate of the site development, materials, labor, equipment and tools, and trade contractor and vendor services needed for its successful completion. No company will survive for long without an accurate and consistent estimating system.

The amount and type of estimating done by builders and remodelers vary. Small volume custom builders may do an estimate for each sales opportunity, whereas builders doing 25 or more homes a year with limited floor plan variations are unlikely to have time to do a detailed estimate for every contract sale. They would just note the differences in feature costs between the two models and use the base cost of the space for the rest.

Estimating methods include the following:

- Rough estimate
- Detailed estimate
- Assembly-based estimate

Rough estimating methods include ballpark square foot estimating, historical estimating, and unit pricing. Rough estimating methods can be used to qualify leads by allowing the estimator to gauge a prospective customer's interest or give a prospective client a reality check without spending a lot of time and effort estimating a project for a non-qualified lead. A quick, rough estimate might increase the odds of closing more projects, but it can lead to problems in under- and over-pricing jobs.

Many builders and remodelers strike a balance between the needs for speed and accuracy, using a rough estimate method to get a commitment for the project with the least amount of work and then creating the detailed estimate to effectively and profitably build the project.

The detailed estimate method involves doing a detailed take-off and bidding out the project) and is time-consuming and potentially expensive, but it yields the most accurate estimate. The detailed estimate method is used for submitting to a client for a custom home or a remodeling project or for planning and setting construction costs for a spec project. The detailed estimate is based on

- Actual bids and quotes from trade contractors and suppliers
- Actual counts for items such as windows and doors, plumbing, and electrical fixtures
- Square foot estimates for siding, finish flooring, drywall, insulation and tile

The detailed estimate provides a comprehensive and defendable estimate and the ability to dis- cover plan and specification errors and inconsistencies.

The detailed estimate is a valuable tool for controlling costs throughout the project. By knowing what the costs should be, any variances discovered during the construction process can be dealt with at the time they occur.

Analysis of a project after its completion can also identify areas where costs were not identified in advance or they were under- or over-estimated. Fine-tuning the estimating system based on actual vs. estimated costs is one of the key aspects of detailed estimating. Storing and maintaining historical budget and budget variance data are critical to developing more accurate estimates. Accurate pricing starts with knowing your direct costs and indirect costs before agreeing to do the work.

Not all projects are good for your company. One of the key benefits of an accurate estimating system is the ability it gives you to identify and evaluate each project for its fit into your business plan. Whether you remodel, build homes on spec, work with owners on a design/build basis or bid on projects as a general contractor, a well-designed and implemented estimating system can help you to determine whether the project is a good fit for your company.

Your Standard Estimating Procedure (SEP) should include the following steps:

Define the Work – The first step in your SEP is to obtain or create the plans, specifications, and scope of work for the project and, if applicable, bidding documents, including the Request for Proposal or Request for Quote and the general conditions for the project being bid.

Assemble Forms and Checklists – The next step in your SEP is to develop consistently accurate estimates and trackable price quotes at the necessary level of detail, your SEP include create forms and checklist to ensure nothing is missed. An example would be your standard line item cost breakdown.

Take-off and Calculations – The next step in your SEP is take-off and calculation. The take-off involves measuring linear footage (LF), square footage and volumes and using those measurements to calculate the actual quantities of labor and materials needed. This step starts with carefully review- ing the plans and specifications and noting key information regarding the scope of work followed by:

- Calculating the costs for each line item. Estimate materials and labor in the same line item as sub-items. Show calculations or bids corresponding to the final numbers to enable tracking to their sources.
- Obtaining current unit pricing from your subcontractors who use unit pricing.
- Obtaining current material pricing from your suppliers.
- Sending out Requests for Proposals (RFP's) or Requests for Quotes (RFQ's) to your sub- contractors who provide lump sum and turnkey pricing, comparing their bids and quotes, and verifying that they include everything that was requested.
- Keeping notes for the schedule identifying tasks that may have a new sequence or explain- ing when time for the task differs from your normal procedure.
- Compiling and reviewing the takeoff.

Compile and Create the Cost Breakdown – The next step in your SEP is compiling and creating the cost breakdown. The cost breakdown, sometimes called a schedule of values, is an organized and logical compilation of all the costs of the project. It is the basis for the job budget where the actual job costs will be gathered and compared to the estimated costs. Typically, it is laid out in sections that generally follow the flow of construction.

I recommend that small volume builders and remodelers use the NAHB Construction Costs Subsidiary Ledger for their cost breakdown. The NAHB cost codes follow the logical sequence of a home building or remodeling the project.

Use the same format that you will use when you track the costs. Keep the level of detail of the cost codes relevant to how you want to categorize the information and account for it in job costing and keep the subcategory levels at the level of detail you need to justify and defend the estimate.

Include hard costs (direct costs) - the cost of labor, materials, supplies, equipment, transportation, and other incidentals and services required to complete the project. Include non-construction costs like architectural design, engineering, consulting, permitting, temporary utilities, and other costs. Include soft costs (indirect costs) which are costs spread out over several jobs. Include allowances for waste. Factor in contingencies - contingencies for line items that are known to vary consistently and contingency for unknown conditions and events.

Total each section of the cost breakdown. Check and recheck the formulas. Since Production is responsible for controlling costs on jobs, it is suggested that the entire estimate with all backup materials and calculations be given to them for a final review.

Set The Selling Price: The final step in your SEP is to set the selling price. Once the cost breakdown has been completed, determine your selling price using your gross margin strategy as described in Chapter 5.

Automating the take-off process can increase speed and accuracy but care must be taken to ensure the automated procedures are error free or you could end up making the same mistakes repeatedly.

Spreadsheet software enables you to customize your estimating process. It is an invaluable tool to both speed the estimating process and increase accuracy. Also, your customized spreadsheets are excellent tools for making presentations to customers. Microsoft® Excel® is one example of spread- sheet software that can be used as a powerful estimating program.

Computer estimating programs build on spreadsheets to create and utilize databases that hold formulas, unit pricing and material prices. Estimating programs come in two forms:

- Stand-alone programs are estimating programs that only do estimating.
- Integrated programs have an estimating component integrated into an entire management program.

Administration should maintain the files of estimates, update any databases and math functions for proper markup, and coordinate the numbering systems that will allow estimates to fold into job costing.

Records of past estimates are great teaching tools and resources for future projects.

Describe your estimating procedure. Do you create a job budget for each job?

Staffing

The Sales Plan portion of your Marketing and Sales Plan should also describe your marketing and sales staff. The roles in the Sales Function are:

- Marketing Manager
- Social media Director
- Public Relations Director
- Sales Representative / Manager
- Designer
- Estimator

The small volume builder or remodeler often fills most if not all these roles for the company. Which roles do you fill? Are you effective? Do you currently have or are you planning on hiring someone to fill any of these roles? If your plan calls for hiring someone, your staffing plan should include how you intend to recruit and hire them, and how you intend to compensate them.

Do you rely on realtors for your sales? If you are a Builder, your sales staffing plan might include using realtors who specialize in new home sales. If you are a Remodeler, your plan might include using realtors who focus on resales.

Regardless of whether you are the salesperson for your company, have or plan on hiring a salesperson or salespersons, or use realtors, your staffing plan should include a plan for training them. Your plan for training them should begin with educating them about your company, your prod- ucts and services, your Unique Selling Proposition, your competition, and your sales process. The National Association of Home Builders (NAHB) offers several Sales and Marketing courses:

- Marketing & Sales for Building Professionals

- Certified New Home Sales Professional (CSP)
    - CSP I: The Art and Science of Selling
    - CSP II: Understanding New Home Construction
    - CSP III: Selling Skills for New Home Sales Professional
- House Construction as a Selling Tool

If you have hired or plan on hiring a sales person or plan on using a realtor, another NAHB courses which might be beneficial is Basics of Building.

If your target market is the 55+ buyer, you might also consider NAHB's Marketing & Communicating with the Aging in Place Client (CAPS I) course.

Describe your sales staffing plan and training plan.

Sales Process

The Sales Plan portion of your Marketing and Sales Plan should also describe your sales process. Your sales process might include the following phases:

- Welcome
- Discovery
- Assess Your Ability to Ease the Customer's Pain
- Gain Commitment
- Service the Sale

Welcome

The goal of the Welcome phase in your sales process is to build trust, create rapport, and demonstrate expertise. The first step in the Welcome phase is Greeting. Your salesperson who is meeting your customer should know your company, your products and services, your Unique Selling Proposition, and your competition. Greeting should include a form of registration card for gathering information on the customer. Your salesperson should fill out the registration card as they guide the customer through the sales plan. Your salesperson should carry a clipboard to take notes and jot down information that they don't want to forget.

Discovery

One goal of the Discovery phase is to determine where the customer is in the home buying process. Customers are typically categorized as A, B. C, or D prospects based on whether they are Ready, Willing, and Able.

- A-buyers are ready, willing and able and will purchase within 30 days
- B-buyers can become an A buyer within 60 days.
- C-buyers can become a B buyer between 4-6 months.
- D-buyers are not ready, not willing, and not able.

Your sales plan for the Discovery phase should include a list of questions for the salesperson to ask. The questions should be open-probe questions to encourage customers to talk. Open-probe questions cannot be answered with a yes or a no. They begin with Who, What, When, Where, Which, and How. Questions you could use to determine where the customer is in the buying process include:

- "Where do you currently live?"
- "Do you presently rent or own?"
- "How long have you lived there?"
- "Why are you searching for a new home?"
- "How many people will be living in your new home?"
- "Who will be living in your new home?"
- "How many other new homes have you visited?"
- "What did you like or dislike about the homes you have visited?"
- "What location is important to you in your new home?"
- "What type of home are you searching for?"
- "How soon are you interested in moving?"
- "What price range of home are you most comfortable with?"

Your sales plan for the Discovery phase should include having your salesperson practice asking the questions in a conversational context and not in an interrogatory fashion.

Another goal of the Discovery phase is learning the source of the customer's pain. Pain motivates change. Their pain is coming from one or more emotional needs. Emotional needs are culture, convenience, romance, recreation, short term investment, long term investment, security, status, prestige, privacy, family, and lifestyle. Emotional needs can be grouped into key areas. Your sales plan should include a list of questions to help your salesperson uncover the customer's emotional needs.

One key area is Experience. Examples of experience question are

- "Have you ever owned a home before?"
- "How long have you owned your present home?"
- "Have you ever built a house before? or Have you ever remodeled your home before?"
- "How familiar are you with the competition?"

Another key area is Requirements. Often what the customer thinks they need doesn't represent the very best fit for them. The salesperson should use their product knowledge to guide customers through these questions. Besides the typical questions regarding the style of home, the number of bedrooms and bathrooms, etc. examples of open-probe requirements questions are:

- "What's missing in the homes you have seen that you would really want in your new home?"
- "If there was just one thing from your present home you could bring with you to your new home, what would it be?"

A third key area is Urgency. Without a sense of urgency, it is impossible to consummate the sale Examples of urgency questions are:

- "Is your present home on the market?"

- "If you found something that was just perfect today, are you ready to move forward?"
- "What is your timeframe based upon?"
- "May I ask why waiting until spring is better for you?"

A fourth key is Situation. Situation covers everything from a growing family, a pending divorce, health issues, a house that needs to sell, to a decision maker who may not be present. Examples of Situation questions are

- "What prompted you to be in the market for a new home now?"
- "How many homes have you seen; how long have you been looking?"
- "Who will be living in the home with you?"
- "What is your family situation?"

A fifth key is Ability. Ability is about how the customer is going to pay. Examples of ability questions are:

- "What would be the ideal monthly housing payment for you?"
- "Have you spoken to a lender?"
- "What initial investment would you like to make in your next purchase?"

The sixth key is Lifestyle. Lifestyle provides hints as to the customer's motivation. Examples of Lifestyle questions are:

- "What did you like least about the home you are moving from?"
- "What do you like most about the home you are moving from?"
- "What style of home appeals to you?"
- "If you could have your ideal home and location what would that be? Why?"

Assess Your Ability to Ease the Customer's Pain

The goal of the Assess Your Ability to Ease the Customer's Pain phase is to match what your customer wants to your products and services.

Once you have discovered the source of your customer's pain, you will know whether you have a product or service that offers the best possible fit for your customer. Your salesperson owes it to the customer, to themselves, and to your company to be the perfect matchmaker. And if you do not have that perfect fit, you owe it to your prospects to send them where they can find what they are looking for. You'd be surprised at how many referrals flow out of prospects who bought somewhere else, but referred their friends, family, or colleagues to you because of your professionalism in looking out for what was best for them.

Gain Commitment

The goal of the Gain Commitment phase is to overcome objections and close the sale. Objections are a sign of interest. Objections are most often a request for more information or a smokescreen for a condition that you did not uncover. Objections can stall or stop the sales process. Your sales plan should include methods and training for handling objections. NAHB's Certified New Home Sales Professional course, *Selling Skills for New Home Sales* provides a six-step model for handling objections.

1. Listen carefully and don't interrupt
2. Restate by rephrasing the objection using cushioning phrases and power words.
3. Acknowledge the customer's concern without agreeing with the objection.
4. Clarify the objection by asking questions to better understand.
5. Formulate the precise planned response to the objection using the few seconds you've bought by restating and acknowledging.
6. Confirm and resume your presentation.

Whatever the reason, this method for handling objections will succeed almost every time in getting you back on track in the sales process.

Closing is defined as the agreement on the part of the customer to willingly move in a direction that is right for them. The ABC's of closing are "Always Be Closing." You must ask for the sale as many times as it takes to close the sale.

Service The Sale

The Service the Sale phase has two components Follow-up and Follow-through. Follow-up is service before the sale. Follow-through is service after the sale. If service remains high before, during, and after the sale, predictable post-purchase behavior creates the raving fan.

Very few prospects purchase on the first visit. For all the others, good follow-up gets them back in the door. Your sales process should include a follow-up plan. Here is a suggested follow-up plan.

A-buyer (will purchase within thirty days)

- Salesperson sends a thank you note and email immediately after their visit.
- Salesperson makes two calls within seven days after their visit
- Salesperson sends a letter within 14 days after their visit
- Company president sends a letter within 14 days after their visit thanking them for their visit and offering contact information
- Salesperson sends multiple emails or makes multiple calls within 21 days
- Salesperson sends a letter before 30 days.

B-buyer (can become an A buyer within sixty days)

- Salesperson sends a thank you note immediately after their visit
- Salesperson sends two emails within seven days after their visit
- Salesperson makes two calls within 14 days after their visit
- Salesperson sends a letter within 14 days after their visit
- Company president sends a letter within 14 days after their visit thanking them for their visit and offering contact information
- Salesperson sends a letter within 30 days after their visit
- Salesperson sends two emails or makes two calls within six weeks after their visit

- Salesperson sends a letter before 60 days.

C-buyer (can become a B buyer between 4-6 months)

- Salesperson sends a thank you note immediately after their visit
- Salesperson sends two emails within 14 days after their visit
- Salesperson makes two calls within 30 days after their visit
- Salesperson sends a letter and two emails and makes two calls within 6 weeks after their visit
- Company president sends a letter within 6 weeks after their visit thanking them for their visit and offering contact information
- Salesperson sends two emails within three months after their visit
- Salesperson makes two calls within four-and-a-half months after their visit
- Salesperson sends a letter before six months.

D-buyer (not ready, not willing, not able)

- Salesperson sends a thank you note immediately after their visit
- Salesperson sends two emails within 60 days after their visit
- Salesperson makes two calls within 120 days after their visit
- Salesperson sends a letter before six months.
- Ask for a referral.

Your sales process should also include a follow-through plan. Follow-through begins at the home orientation. The home orientation sets buyers' expectations about how to manage their new home. Your home orientation should include the following:

- Explain how to operate the home's major systems and appliances.
- Provide information about care and maintenance of the home's finishes.
- Reduce customer service calls by explaining the most frequent causes of problems and malfunctions.
- Explain the owner's maintenance responsibilities, the builder's warranty procedures and responsibilities, and the differences between the two.
- Provide information about special construction materials, features, or conditions, and the appropriate maintenance measures.
- Verify the home is complete and ready for occupancy.

Your follow-through plan should include a plan for dealing with customers who experience problems after the sale. It should describe how you train new homeowners in warranty procedures and your company's emergency procedures, i.e. whom to call when something goes wrong unexpectedly.

Finally, your follow-through plan should include a questionnaire to solicit comments from your new customers and to ask for referrals and/or testimonials.

Describe your sales process

Sales Center

If you have or intend to have a sales center or showroom, describe it here.

Sales and Revenue Forecast

The Sales and Revenue Forecast section of your Marketing and Sales Plan is where you describe your sales and revenue goals. For builders and remodelers, customer inquiries i.e. leads typically follow this progression:

- Raw leads convert to qualified leads,
- Qualified leads convert to confirmed appointments,
- Appointments convert to proposals, and
- Proposals convert to sales

Your sales goals should include goals for each of those steps.

Percentage of Raw Leads That Convert to Qualified Leads Goal

Not all the leads your marketing generates will be qualified leads. Of the top 25% of Remodelers Advantage Roundtable Members, the average percentage of their raw leads that converted to qualified leads was 59%. A qualified lead is a lead that turns into an appointment. Your Sales and Revenue Forecast should include a goal for the percentage of raw leads that convert to qualified leads.

Percentage of Appointments That Convert to Proposals Goal

As noted in the Sales Process section, your products and services might not be a perfect fit for every customer with whom you meet.

Percentage of Appointments That Convert to Sales Goal

The percentage of appointments that convert to sales is your Closing Ratio. The number of contracts divided by the number of qualified leads multiplied by 100 is your closing ratio expressed as a percent. If, for example, your lead generation strategy generated 50 qualified leads and those leads resulted in 10 signed contracts, your closing ratio is 10 divided by 50 multiplied by 100, which equals 20 percent. Of the top 25% of Remodelers Advantage Roundtable Members, the average number of qualified leads that turn into construction contracts was 1 out of 5 or 20%.

Sales Goal

For builders and remodelers, your sales goal will be expressed as the number of contracts signed per month or per year.

Revenue Goal

Your revenue goal is your average product price multiplied by you sales goal.

If developed and implemented properly, your Marketing and Sales plan will have a high probability of success. If properly built and utilized, it will produce continuous improvements and a competitive advantage.

Now that you've defined your target market and your products and services and developed your marketing and sales plan, the next step in writing your business plan is to develop your operations plan – how you are going to manage the administrative operations of the company and how you are going to produce the deliver the products and services your sales staff sells.

CHAPTER 7

OPERATIONS PLAN

"Good management consists in showing average people how to do the work of superior people."

—John D. Rockefeller

Remember the six P's necessary to the success of any business discussed in Chapter 2? The Operations Plan section of your business plan is where you discuss Process. It is where you describe the systems and procedures.

The National Association of Home Builders "Business Management for Building Professionals" course identifies the three functional areas of a company as

- Sales
- Administration
- Production

The Marketing and Sales Plan described the Sales function. The Operations Plan is where you'll describe the systems and procedures you use to insure the Administration and Production functions operate efficiently and effectively. Although the three areas are distinct, there are also many overlaps, especially in the areas of sales and customer service. Teamwork is essential as are shared goals. All employees should be encouraged to recognize and appreciate the roles that others play

The roles in the Administration function are:

- Business planning and budgeting
- Setting up and maintaining company processes
- Bookkeeping
- Processing payables and receivables
- Estimating
- Job Costing
- Setting up and maintaining computer systems, like accounting software, contact management and project management systems
- Working with advisors such as accountant, insurance agent, attorney, and banker
- Creating and maintaining the employee handbook
- Performing role of receptionist

- Communicating with all stakeholders

The roles in the Production function are

- Scheduling
- Purchasing
- Managing field employees and subcontractors
- Keeping the job on schedule
- Controlling costs
- Preparing and reacting to job cost variance reports
- Communicating progress to customers, the office, the sales team, bankers, and key stakeholders
- Producing a quality job that is profitable and earns your customer's satisfaction
- Vetting new products and adding those that safely maintain the company's reputation
- Safety

Administration

Staffing

The roles in the Administration function include:

- General Manager
- Office Manager
- Secretary / Administrative Assistant
- Receptionist
- Bookkeeper / Accountant
- Customer Service Manager
- Human Resource Director
- Computer / IT Expert

Most small volume builders or remodelers will not have individuals in each of these roles. Employees might fill several roles. The General Manager might also fill the role of estimator and customer service manager. The office manager might also fill the roles of secretary/administrative assistant, receptionist, and bookkeeper.

Describe your present Administration staffing.

Describe your plans for adding staff.

Bookkeeping and Processing Payables and Receivables

Chart of Accounts

A chart of accounts (COA) is a list of the accounts used by a business to categorize and capture financial information. NAHB has created a Chart of Accounts for the home building industry. The chart assigns a numeric code to label each entry found on an income statement or balance sheet. The code helps with the process of putting items in the correct financial category and in a logical order. NAHB's COA can be found at nahb.org.

Describe the chart of accounts your company uses.

Accounting Method

Cash accounting is the easiest accounting method to use because it only records cash exchanges. It reports revenues, costs and expenses in the accounting period in which the cash was physically received or disbursed, regardless of when the revenues were earned or the expenses incurred. The disadvantages to cash accounting are due to the potential time lag between when revenues are earned and cash is received, or when expenses are incurred and actually paid. Because of this potential time lag, financial statements will not accurately reflect the most current financial condition. It does help for tax management, however.

Accrual accounting recognizes revenues when they are earned and expenses when they are incurred, regardless of when the cash is received or paid out. On the income side, when an invoice is given to a customer, the revenue is recognized even if payment has not been received. Similarly, on the expense side, when an invoice is received, it is immediately recognized in the system even though payment is not made until later; it is logged as an accounts payable item, a current liability.

The accrual method of accounting presents a more current picture of the financial condition of the company than the cash accounting method.

Two permutations of accrual accounting are:

Completed contract accounting – This is often used by builders and contractors doing jobs that span multiple year ends. It delays a taxable event until the project is actually closed or sold.

Percent complete accounting – This accounting allows you to take in revenue at the same pace as you recognize expected costs as compared to total costs. It says that if you incurred 25 percent of the expected costs to perform a job, then you are entitled to take 25 percent of the total anticipated revenues, and not a penny more or less. Accounting entries are made to bring the income accounts back in line with the percent complete for a given period. After the reports are run, the entries are reversed and life goes on in accrual until the next month end when the process occurs again.

Percent complete accounting takes a little time; it takes a little more accuracy in estimates; and it takes some accounting background or a macro for the few accounts that require entries. But it is absolutely the only managerially sound accounting system for a company to truthfully reflect profitability at a single point in time.

Describe the accounting method do you use.

Job Costing

Job costing is important to maintain consistent profitability. It enables you to compare your estimated and actual costs on a weekly or monthly basis, identify variances, determine the reasons for the variances, and take corrective action.

Job Cost Budget

The job cost budget is created from the estimate. Like the estimate, the job cost budget lists all the job costs by category or construction phase — like foundation, framing, plumbing, drywall and paint.

The job cost budget should be provided to the Production staff to establish benchmarks for their efficiency and effectiveness.

Job Cost Reporting

Recording job costs is a critical accounting responsibility. A job cost report is a monitoring tool for both Administration and Production. As construction progresses and invoices come in, costs for each category for each individual job should be recorded. Job cost reports can be generated weekly or monthly and allow the relatively current monitoring and analysis of actual job costs versus the estimated job costs. Both positive and negative variances represent deviations. Use the job cost budget to see if the job is tracking well and, if not, ask yourself what can be done to save it. If problems are identified and addressed early, many jobs can be saved by changing a supplier, negotiating harder, changing staffing to less expensive or more productive workers, or pricing change orders more aggressively. If it cannot be saved, at least learn how you can make the next job estimate and produced job more profitable.

Accurately recording all job costs and creating a job cost report can provide a builder or remodeler with the following benefits:

- The ability to track and control costs during the building/remodeling job (Using work orders for subcontractors and purchase orders for materials, you are able to view the costs that have been incurred to date and the costs that remain in each of the cost categories and project the financial health of a project at any time and how it will end up.)
- The ability to view areas of work that consistently run over budget, underestimated budgeted costs or, worse, forgotten items.
- The ability to create a databank so that future job cost estimates can build on previous experiences and margin slippage, and be more accurate.
- The ability to detect fraud by watching incoming costs in real time (Organizations lose an estimated 5 percent of their annual revenues due to fraud.)
- A mini profit and loss report to see whether your gross profit margin for the whole company is tracking well

Describe your systems and procedures for preparing job cost reports. How often do you produce job cost reports?

How do you react to variances in job costs?

Production

Staffing

The roles in the Production function include:

- Project Manager
- Scheduler
- Purchaser
- Superintendent
- Lead Carpenter
- Crew Foremen

As with the Accounting function, most small volume builders or remodelers will not have individuals in each of these Production roles. Employees might fill several roles. The project manager might also fill the roles of scheduler, purchaser, and superintendent. Or the superintendent might also fill the role of lead carpenter.

Describe your present production staffing.

Do you have a Project Manager? What are his/her responsibilities? How many projects is he/ she responsible for? How is he/she compensated?

Do you have a Scheduler? What are his/her responsibilities? How is he/she compensated? Do you have a Purchaser? What are his/her responsibilities? How is he/she compensated?

Do you have a Superintendent? What are his/her responsibilities? How many projects is he/she responsible for? How is he/she compensated?

Do you have your own crews? Describe them. Describe your training programs.

Describe any anticipated changes as the company grows.

Purchasing

Your Operations Plan should include policies and procedures for purchasing. The use of subcon- tracts and work orders for trade contractors and purchase orders for materials limits the slippage in job costs.

Your policies and procedures for awarding subcontracts should include

- Checking the contractor's license or registration, if applicable

- Checking the contractor's reputation with other builders or remodelers
- Checking the contractor's credit
- Checking the contractor's insurance
- Obtaining the contractor's W-9

In addition to the subcontractor's price, work orders should include a description of the subcontractor's scope of work, copies of the specifications, and scheduled dates for the work to be performed.

In addition to a description of the materials, the quantities, and the prices, purchase orders should include the scheduled dates for delivery of the material and lead times for ordering.

Scheduling

Scheduling is the complement to estimating. The schedule is the time estimate for the project. Time is a key ingredient to profitability for Builders and Remodelers. Whether the schedule is for the in-house labor or a project with all subcontractors, it is the controlling document to keep the project on track. The estimate becomes the budget; the schedule will complete the project as planned.

Even though time is a key element to their profitability, when asked about scheduling construction activities, almost 24% of the builders and remodelers questioned reported that they did not have any formal scheduling procedures of any kind.

The schedule is a list of activities that leads to a desired outcome or conclusion of a unique project. In home building and remodeling, an effective schedule organizes project activities from start to finish in a sequence that ensures they are performed logically and efficiently.

A schedule is not a schedule until it is documented or until it is printed. It is primarily a communication tool and if it is not written down or printed, it compromises its effectiveness for fulfilling that purpose.

There are several types of schedules:

- Handwritten schedule
- Calendar schedule
- Spreadsheet schedule
- Computerized schedule

When asked about scheduling construction activities, just under 73% of the builders and remodelers questioned said they used "daily to-do lists" as their primary method, just over 11% said they used simple bar charts, and 18% said they used computerized scheduling programs.

Creating the project might seem like a daunting task but the benefit is from the process of thinking through the project. To be useful, a schedule requires a significant amount of information and careful thought. Once a schedule has been created, it often can be copied, modified and repurposed for other jobs. The key to creating an effective schedule is to use a systematic approach that incorporates all of the basic parts of a schedule matched with known job factors, Builder or Remodeler experience, and reasonable forecasting.

Any construction project can be a complex process fraught with decisions, selections, unforeseen conditions and problems that can have severe impact on its success. Communication becomes the lifeblood for efficient work flow and problem solving.

The project schedule can help communicate this complexity to the project team members in a way that facilitates their successful participation and contribution to the project goals. The project schedule needs to be concise, to the point, timely, and documented.

A schedule is a picture of a project and its steps to completion. It illustrates each task and the relationships among tasks. This contributes to the communication process in several ways:

- Clarifies accountability – it communicates to all team members their responsibilities and their impact on others.
- Encourages planning – To complete a project in a timely manner every team member must look forward to their next task. The schedule is a tool for encouraging team members' planning and preparation for executing their upcoming project tasks in a timely manner.
- Supports efficiency – One of the biggest frustrations of trade contractors is being told that their work is ready when it is not. The result is lost time, energy and profits from not being able to do their task efficiently. Each task in a schedule has definitive start and finish dates, which minimizes these frustrations and emphasizes on-time completion as well.
- Promotes teamwork – When projects run into unforeseen difficulties and you need to make up time, the modified schedule with the input from the team will solidify efforts to get the project back on track.
- Promotes business success – A complete and well-managed schedule helps trade contractors run their individual businesses more efficiently. Builders and Remodelers that effectively manage their subcontractors and suppliers with schedules find that their trade partners are more likely to give their projects priority over competitors without communicated schedules.

A schedule cannot benefit a project until it is published and distributed to all of the parties involved in the project:

- For Custom Builders and Remodelers, design professionals must receive it to be educated on the impact of the decisions they and their clients make.
- All subcontractors must receive it to know their anticipated start time, completion date, timeline, whom they are dependent on, and who is dependent on them.
- Suppliers must receive it so they understand when to order materials and insure their delivery when they are needed.
- Project Managers must be assured that the schedule provides an accurate sequence of the upcoming activities and has integrity as a planning tool.
- Company production crews must receive it to know their anticipated start time, completion date, timeline, whom they are dependent on, and who is dependent on them.
- Administration staff must receive it in order to assist Production in the coordination of the project.
- Upper management needs the schedule to see at a glance where the project stands.
- Sales staff should receive it so they are informed of the projects status

Custom Builders and Remodelers should also distribute the schedule to clients. Providing clients with a copy of the schedule and reviewing it with them points out to clients the need for their timely decisions and the impact their decisions have on task dependencies and shows clients the relationship between their decision dates and the related tasks to help facilitate their decisions. It can also be used to hold clients responsible for completing their decisions by their decision dates. Builders and Remodelers should consider scheduling these decision dates as far in advance as possible. The schedule can also be used to illustrate to the client the impact of their requests for changes and delivery delays associated with longer lead items and out of stock items.

To be truly effective as a communication tool, the information represented in the schedule must be accurate:

- Information must accurately represent the actual project status.
- It must be updated regularly to ensure that current job information is posted.
- Updates need to be provided to all team members so they can react and plan accordingly and perform their work in a timely and profitable manner.

When asked about their scheduling activities, builders and remodelers who reported using some type of scheduling program, 29.4% of the respondents updated schedules only monthly, while 42.6% updated weekly, and 27.9% updated their schedules daily.

All builders and remodelers will benefit from using schedules to manage the many aspects of their projects and integrating communication practices with the schedule.

Describe your scheduling system and procedures.

- **What method of scheduling do you use?**
- **Is it used primarily for in-house labor or on projects with subcontractors?**
- **How is it distributed?**
- **How often is updated?**

Quality Control Plan

Your Operations Plan should include a Quality Control Plan. Delivering a quality product and experience produces higher margins, fewer call backs, and increased reputation which results in more referrals and repeat customers.

Quality is a process. It is the result of ongoing dedication and commitment. Distinguishing yourself from the competition with well-documented Quality Control systems and procedures that reflect your company's goals and standards in all that you do is key to developing your reputation as being a quality builder or remodeler.

Quality is defined two ways—internally and externally. The internal definition is how you define your products and services. The external definition is how your customers and others outside of your organization perceive the quality of your products and services. Consumers today view quality as a given and not as a bonus that they receive for a wise purchase. Customers today are more sophisticated than ever and expect more quality for their money. This quality equates to perceived value in their eyes. You can reinforce the perception of quality through the use of a system that relies on written, well-defined, measurable quality controls supported by forms, checklists and inspection reports.

Quality control is a team effort. Your team includes your employees – sales and administrative staff as well as your production staff. The vast majority of builders and some remodelers subcontract most, if not all, of their work so your team also includes your subcontracts and suppliers. Your customers typically view your subcontractors as employees. And your team also includes your customer. Your Quality Control should focus on accurate and complete documentation. Accurate and complete documentation is key to communicating your expectations to your team members. Documentation includes your promotional material; your sales agreements; your plans and specifications; your subcontracts, work orders, and purchase orders; your selection sheets, your quality control checklists, your home orientation forms, etc.

An essential element of your quality control plan is well prepared construction documents. Construction documents should be produced for each project and should be specific to that project. Your construction documents should include your customer's name and address in all of the blocks to emphasize how important the customer is to our company. Don't use a standard plan marked-up to reflect your customer's specific modifications. Construction documents should include:

- Plans in sufficient detail to accurately depict the finished product to all team members. Plans should include the Site Plan, Floor Plans, Structural Plans including Foundation and Framing Plans as applicable, Mechanical Plans, Electrical Plans, and Architectural and Structural Details.
- Specifications that clearly and accurately define the scope of work for all team members. Specifications can be a sheet on the plans or a separate document.
- Your Sales Agreement that defines your responsibilities and those of your customer
- Change Orders
- Job specific Subcontracts, Work Orders, and Purchase Orders
- Your warranty documents.

Another essential element of your quality control plan is clearly defined written quality standards. The purpose of quality standards is to define what quality means to you. Clearly defined quality standards communicate your definition of quality to your employees and subcontractors and enable you to evaluate their work.

Builders and remodelers have all experience the problems that can occur because of failing to account for lead times when ordering materials, ordering the incorrect materials (not what was specified), not informing all the affected team member of changes, or having to perform work out of sequence because subcontractors or materials were not available when required by the schedule. These problems may occur more often than you would like to admit, but the real quality nemesis is poor craftsmanship. These types of problems, even if eventually resolved, can negatively impact your customer's perception of quality. The selection of quality-minded subcontractors and customer-service oriented suppliers can help avoid these problems. Quality-minded subcontractors not only perform their work correctly and in a timely manner, they also do not cover up any poor workmanship that preceded their work. While the role of project management is prevent or at least mitigate the occurrence of these problems, quality standards for employees, subcontractors, and suppliers can help.

Quality standards for your employees should include:

- Standards for qualifying subcontractors and suppliers
- Standard for awarding subcontracts and work orders
- Standards for selecting, purchasing and delivery of materials
- Standards for scheduling projects

Because builders and remodelers rely heavily on subcontractors and suppliers, it is essential that they understand and support your total quality effort. Treat them as team members. Explain to them that a quality project benefits them as well as you. Explain how a quality project can lower their cost, increased their profitability, and result in more referral work. Solicit their input on what can be done better.

Quality standards for subcontractors and suppliers supplement your project specific specifications and should be included in every subcontract, work order and purchase order. These standards typically include the following:

- Job site protocol
- Courtesy to the homeowner
- Communication with the homeowner
- Jobsite Cleanup policy (i.e. Job to be left broom clean at the end of each day)
- No loud music or profanity
- No smoking policy
- Job site waste management (i.e. All trash and debris to be placed in receptacle at the end of each day.)
- Job site work hours
- Do not use anything that belongs to the customer or a neighboring resident
- Observe all local, state, and OSHA regulations
- Acceptable material standards
- Minimum performance standards of systems
- Acceptable tolerances for square, level and plumb.
- Acceptable finish tolerances for interior trim, drywall, etc.
- Standard details for exterior and interior elements such as trim, molding, corners, etc.
- Your policy for paying for work only after it has been completed to your satisfaction.
- Your policies and procedures regarding warranty - their responsibilities and your expectations regarding response times.

For small to medium volume builders and remodelers, the "Residential Construction Performance Guidelines" published by NAHB is an excellent reference for developing your minimum performance standards.

Your quality control plan should also include quality control tools. Include checklists for each stage of construction. Besides insuring that work is completed according to your standards, check lists can have another benefit. Employees observed by the customers using these checklists are perceived as well-trained and thorough. Customers tend to view themselves as your "Quality Control Helpers." Their input should be welcome throughout construction. Reviewing your quality control checklists with your customer and letting them know what you are looking for will encourage them to watch for the same things and might divert their attention away from other things. Reviewing these checklists with your customer can also instill his confidence in the completed project.

On the other hand, if the customer is involved in identifying defective work, your reputation can suffer. Another quality control tool you should consider including is a "Red Tag" system. Your employees should never walk by defective work. A "Red Tag" system allows them to identify the defect. The red tag should clearly state that your company has identified the defect and is taking action to correct it. If your customer does identify a defect before you or your employees and notifies you, they should be responded to promptly and every effort should be made to correct it the same day. If your customer feels ignored or believes a problem would not have been corrected if they had not caught it, they might start to believe that they must supervise their project daily and your reputation for doing quality work will suffer. On the other hand, if your customer sees your red tags and sees that problems are being corrected promptly, you will build a solid relationship and boost your customer's confidence in the finished product.

Your quality control program should also include ongoing training programs for employees and subcontractors. The National Association of Home Builders (NAHB) offers a number of courses:

- Basics of Building
- Building Technology: Systems and Interior Finishes
- Building Technology: Structures and Exterior Finishes
- House Construction As A Selling Tool
- Project Management
- Customer Service, and
- Profitable Business Through Quality Practices

Last but certainly not least, your Quality Control Plan MUST include a process and procedure for educating your customer. Your customer must understand what they are purchasing.

More and more, customers are demanding that your product be closer to the elusive "perfect home." Immediately after signing the sales agreement, the builder or remodeler and the customer appear to be on the same page. It's what happens after that lights the fire of controversy. Homeowner lawsuits, mediations and arbitrations are often initiated over conflicting opinions of cosmetic issues and items that builders and remodelers refer to as "standard in the industry".

Educating your customer begins with understanding their expectations. Customer education should be initiated as early in the process as possible and should continue throughout the planning and construction process. The goal of your construction education process is discovering your customer's expectations, address their expectations, and guide them to realistic, achievable expectations. One way to educate your customer and help shape their expectation is to provide them with a list of your past customers.

Pre-Construction Conference

Your customer education process should begin with a Pre-Construction Conference. During the Pre-Conference you should ask open-probe questions to encourage your customer to discuss their expectations. You should introduce the production staff and explain their roles and responsibilities. The Pre-Construction Conference should include reviewing the construction agreement with them to insure they have a clear understanding of their roles and responsibilities as well as yours.

Your construction agreement should address the following:

- Your payment schedule
- Your change order procedures (i.e. change requests must be in writing to the builder or remodeler, change requests must be made before a certain stage in construction, etc.)
- Your warranty and warranty service request procedure
- Termination/arbitration/mediation dispute resolution procedures.
- Restrictions on direct communication with subcontractors and supplier
- Your safety policy as it relates to visits to the construction site (i.e. homeowner must wear a hard hat and safety glasses, homeowner should only visit the site during normal working hours unless accompanied by the builder or remodeler, etc.)

The Pre-Construction Conference should also include a review of the completed plans and specification with the customer to ensure that they understand the product to be delivered. Explain construction terms, symbols, and measurements terms so your customer can examine the plans with clarity and understanding. Require customers to sign and date each page of the plans before the start of a project. If the specifications are a separate document from the plans, review the specifications with them, have them initial and date each page and sign the last page. When drawings and specifications are properly explained to the customer, they will appreciate your efforts to minimize errors and confusion. If available, include pictures and copies of manufacturer's brochures when describing fixtures and equipment. The signed and dated plans and specifications should become part of the construction agreement. They can be used to settle misunderstandings, non-compliance issues and quality standard disputes.

The Pre-Construction Conference should also include a review of the project schedule. The review should walk the customer through all the phases of the construction process from site work to foundation to framing to system rough-ins to drywall to interior finishes to home-owner orientation. It should identify the subcontractor responsible for each phase, if known, and include an explanation of what the customer should expect during each phase. If the schedule contains milestones for customer decisions or walk-throughs, they should be addressed. It also means, wherever possible, creating realistic, achievable expectations through education and guidance.

The Pre-Construction Conference should briefly discuss the other elements of your quality control plan.

Finally, the Pre-Construction Conference should describe your warranty process and procedures. Builders and remodelers typically define the quality of their product by the quality of the design, workmanship, and materials used. Their evaluation of product quality typically takes into consideration foundation design, structural framing, mechanical installations, insulation and other elements. However, the customer may not appreciate how these elements contribute to a quality product.

Homeowners often measure quality by evaluating items that builders and remodelers regard as relatively minor, such as:

- Switch or plug plates out of level
- A squeak in the floor
- Wall and ceiling finishes that are slightly out of square
- Hairline cracks in caulking, tile grout or mortar joints
- Visible carpet or vinyl flooring seams
- Sheetrock patches improperly blended with a wall surface

While many subjective elements of a home are legitimately irrelevant to the home's underlying integrity and performance, they do represent quality, or the lack of it, in the mind of the average homeowner.

Your customer education process MUST educate your customer about the features which you use to define quality. But they must be presented to the customer in terms of the advantages and benefits they provide.

A well-documented, customer-centered quality control system and procedures will set you apart from your competition. A customer-centered approach to quality means that your customer can answer "Yes" to the following questions:

- Do I have a clear picture of what my project will look like upon completion? And does my contractor share that picture?
- Has my contractor supplied working drawings and elevations, as well as a complete proposal including specifications and agreement?

- Do I have a clear understanding of the construction period and of the variables that can affect it?
- Has my contractor provided me with a payment schedule?
- Do I understand the contractor's warranty program, and what, if any, published quality standards he or she subscribes to?
- Has my contractor provided names of previous clients?
- Have all of my questions been answered to my satisfaction?

Sharing your quality standards with prospective home buyers can also be an excellent marketing tool.

Some customers never truly believe that their home was built right so your Quality Control Plan might include procedures for dealing with unhappy customers with the goal of turning them around and regaining their confidence. Such procedures might include early damage control in the form of personal attention and a willingness to correct problems quickly.

Describe your quality control system and procedures.

Safety Plan

Statistically, home building and remodeling is the most dangerous industry. It is included in your business plan because it can impact your profitability. Safety should be a consideration when estimating every project. A poor safety reputation can generate bad publicity. But it can seriously impact your project budgets. Consider:

- The cost of shutting down for accidents, injuries, and near-misses
- The cost of citations
- The cost of increased insurance premiums or loss of insurance coverage
- The effect of a fatality on the company

The three reasons for job site safety are humanitarian, economic, and legal.

The primary reason to enforce safety throughout your company and in any company working with you is because you care about your employees, your subcontractors, and their employees. The people who work for you are a valuable resource and you should protect them!

On an average 2,000-square foot house, the cost of workers compensation insurance covering your workers and the employees of the subcontractors is $4,321.

OSHA fines can range from $500 to $300,000 on a single residential project.

Increasing medical and insurance costs, coupled with high compensatory and punitive damages awarded to workers, job site visitors, and others injured, disabled, or killed on construction job sites have resulted in tremendous potential liability.

Your Safety plan should include the following:

- Company Safety Policy Statement
- Program Safety Goals and Objectives
- Organizational Safety Responsibilities- Designate a "safety coordinator/champion" even if that person has other duties.

- General Safety Rules - Identify common job site hazards and develop policies and procedures to address those hazards.
- Hazard Communication
- Lock Out, Tag Out
- Confined Space Entry Policies and Training (where applicable)
- Subcontractors - Require that all subcontractors have an effective, working safety program in place.
- Safety Education and Training
- Internal Safety Inspections
- OSHA Inspection Procedures
- Accident Investigation
- Recordkeeping and Documentation
- Emergency Action Plan
- Disaster Planning
- First Aid
- Substance Abuse, and
- Enforcement, Discipline, Reward Program

Describe your safety program.

You've defined your target market and your products and services. You've developed your marketing and sales plan and your operations plan. The next step in writing your business plan is to describe your company's leadership team – your current leadership, your plans for adding members to your leadership team, and your plans for developing and training your company's leaders.

CHAPTER 8

LEADERSHIP TEAM AND STAFFING PLAN

"In the end, all business operations can be reduced to three words: people, product and profits. Unless you've got a good team, you can't do much with the other two."

—Lee Iacocca

Leadership Team

The adage is that investors don't invest in ideas, they invest in people. Some investors even go as far as to say that they would rather invest in a mediocre idea with a great team behind it than a block- buster idea with a mediocre team.

What this really means is that running a successful business all comes down to execution. Can you accomplish what you have planned? Do you have the right team in place to turn a good idea into a great business that will have customers banging down your doors?

The Leadership Team and Staffing Plan chapter of your business plan is where you make your best case that you have the right team in place to execute on your idea. The Leadership Team and Staffing Plan chapter also shows that you have thought about the important roles and responsibilities your business needs to grow and be successful.

Remember the three functional areas of a company and the roles in each function. Each of those roles must be filled for a business to be successful. And as we have noted in previous chapters, the small volume builder or remodeler often fills multiple roles in the company. This may be due to lack of additional skilled resources or other financial considerations, your unwillingness to lose control through delegation, or your inability to let go of the parts of the business that are familiar and enjoyable. You need to honestly assess your personal strengths and weaknesses. If you try to fill too many roles, especially roles for which you are not qualified or roles you don't really enjoy, you run the risk of not being able to handle any of the related responsibilities well. You will sacrifice time and energy you could better spend performing the tasks that are most important and appropriate for you.

You don't have to know everything about business - but you do need a basic understanding of the systems and standard operating procedures that are required for your business - to function and survive. For builders and remodelers, these systems are accounting, estimating, and job scheduling.

Since you probably fill several of the leadership roles in your company, your Leadership Team and Staffing Plan chapter should include your brief bio. Your bio should highlight your industry experience and education. If you have earned any professional designations or industry awards, highlight them, and be sure to include a description of the designation or award for those who might not be familiar with it.

Include the bios of any other leadership team members.

Leadership Staffing Plan

Your leadership team doesn't necessarily need to be complete to have a complete business plan. If you know that you have gaps in your leadership team, that's OK. If you have gaps in your team, simply identify them and briefly describe your plan for filling those roles. Include the qualifications and your timetable for filling the role. If you are writing an external business plan, lenders and investors will see the fact that you know you are missing certain key people as a sign of maturity and knowledge about what your business needs to succeed.

Finally, you might include a proposed organizational chart in your business plan. This isn't critical and can be included as a figure in the Leadership and Staffing Plan section or as an appendix. An organizational chart is a useful planning tool to help you think about your company and how it will grow over time. What key roles will you be looking to fill in the future and how will you structure your teams to get the most out of them? An org chart can help you think through these questions. If you are seeking funding, you may be asked for an "org chart," so it's good to have one.

Here is an example of a simple organization chart for a small volume builder or remodeler.

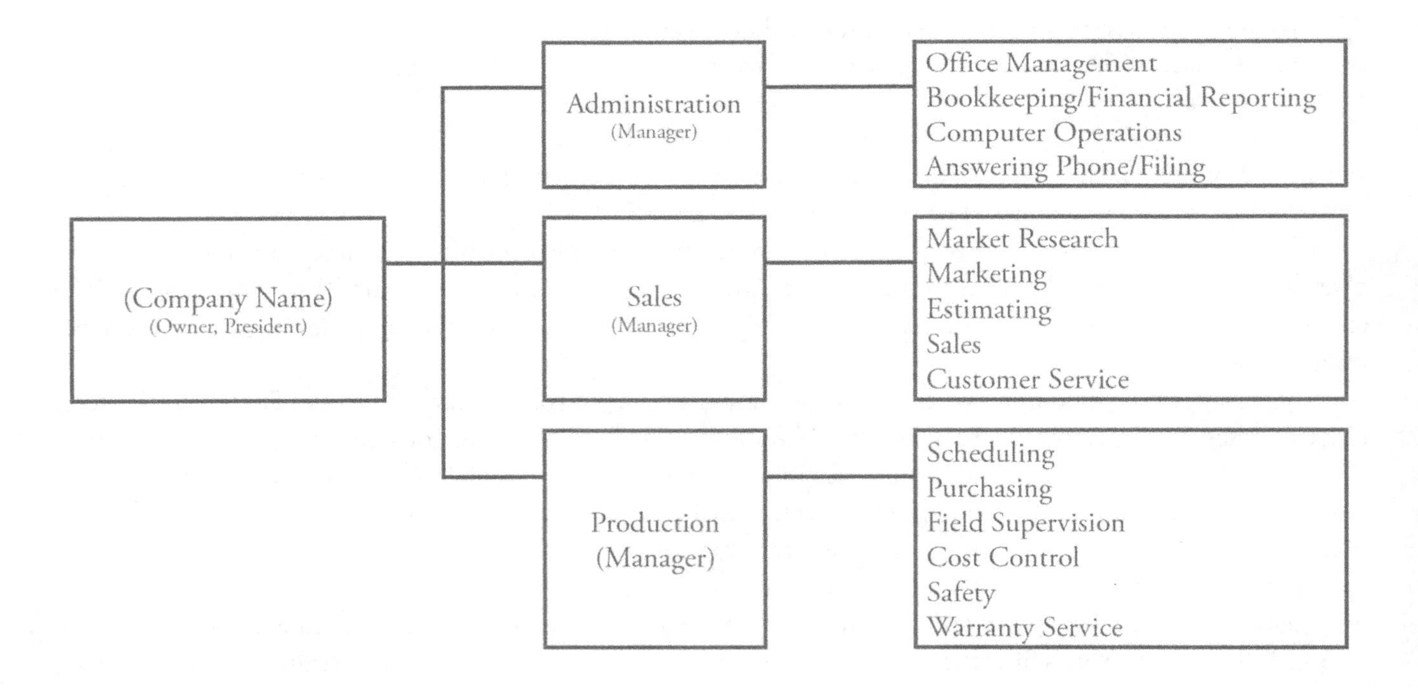

Leadership Development Plan

Describe your plans for developing the leadership, management and technical skills, and capabilities of your current leadership staff – including yourself - in their range of roles and areas of responsibility.

Describe the training and development programs in use.

Describe how you are presently assessing, developing, or planning to develop leaders and managers to fuel the growth of the organization in the coming 12 to 36 months.

Succession Plan

If you anticipate transitions in ownership or leadership during the next five years, you should also describe your succession plan. Is there a member or members of your existing leadership team that are interested in acquiring the company?

You've defined your target market and your products and services. You've developed your marketing and sales plan and your operations plan, and you've described your company's leadership team. The next step in writing your business plan is to write your goals and develop action plans for achieving them.

CHAPTER 9

GOALS AND ACTION PLANS

"People with goals succeed because they know where they're going."

—Earl Nightingale

While the Goals and Action Plans chapter of your business plan may not be long, it's critical that you take the time to write down your goals.

Goals "held" in your mind are more likely to be jumbled up with the other 1500 thoughts per minute the average human being experiences. Writing our goals down forces us to avoid being vague. The act of writing down a goal is a very powerful motivator.

Here are some goal setting facts and figures:

According to USA Today, only 4% of people who do NOT write their goals down actually follow through on them.

Studies by Gail Matthews at Dominican University in California have proven that strategies for effective goal achievement include writing goals down and sharing goals. In 2007, Dr. Matthews did a study of students who tracked goal achievement comparing groups who wrote down their goals to those who didn't. She found that students who wrote down their goals were 42% more likely to achieve them.

Sharing your goals with a close confidante is proven to increase the chances of you achieving your goal.

A University of Virginia study found that people who write down their goals earn nine times more money over their lifetime than people who don't.

If you are seeking funding, bankers and potential investors will want to see that you understand what needs to happen to make your plans a reality, and that you are working on a realistic schedule.

Goals

Your goals need to be SMART.

Specific: Set specific goals that use real numbers and deadlines. "I want more visitors" doesn't cut it. "I want 25 new leads at the end of each month" is the kind of goal you're after.

Measurable: Don't hide behind vague buzz words like "brand engagement" or "social influence." Make sure you can measure and track your progress. Your goals should detail the key metrics that you will be watching. Metrics are the numbers that you watch on a regular basis to judge the health of your business and track the growth of your business. These could include the number of sales leads generated, the number of page views to your website, or any other critical metric that helps determine the health of your business. They are the drivers of growth for your business model and your financial plan.

Attainable: Set goals you can reach. Doubling your leads in one week won't happen.

Realistic: Be honest with yourself. Consider hurdles and obstacles you'll face and be honest about what you and your team are truly capable of.

Time-bound: Set a specific (and hard) deadline. Without a specific deadline, you'll just keep pushing tasks out.

Your goals should include short term (next 12 months), intermediate (next 2 to 3 years), and long term (5 to 10 years) goals for your company. You should have already established some of your goals in the Products and Services Plan, Marketing and Sales Plan, Operations Plan, and Leadership Team and Staffing sections of your business plan, so some of your work has already been done. Just carry those goals forward to this section.

You should establish goals in each of the three functional areas – Administration, Sales, and Production. Your work on your business plan thus far should have revealed several areas for improvement. Here are some suggestions:

Administration goals might include adding or upgrading your accounting software, adding staff, developing a company policies and procedures manual, and developing an employee handbook. Sales goals might include upgrading your website, increasing your social media marketing, acquiring customer relationship management (CRM) software, acquiring estimating software,

increasing sales, adding staff, and increasing your gross margin on projects.

Depending on your current situation, your sales goals might also include adding a sales center, showroom, or model home.

Production goals might include decreasing slippage, increasing quality, and increasing safety. Depending on your current staffing, production goals might include adding a project manager, superintendent, scheduling engineer, and/or purchaser.

Depending on your current policies and procedures, production goals might also include acquiring new scheduling software; creating a standard subcontract agreement, standard trade contractor scopes of work, and standard work order forms; and implementing a purchase order system. Depending on your current operations, production goals might also include diversification.

If you are a builder, your goals might include adding remodeling. If you only build your standard plans, your goals might include adding custom building. If you are a custom builder, your goals might include adding standard plans. If you are a remodeler, your goals might include adding a specialty like remodeling for aging-in-place. Residential builders and remodelers might include a goal to add commercial and/or institutional projects to your products and services.

Describe your top 5 short-term goals for the company for the next 12 months.

Describe your top 5 intermediate-term goals for the company for the next 2 to 3 years.

Finally, describe your top 5 long-term goals for the company for the next 5 to 10 years.

Action Plans

Every SMART goal must be complemented by a detailed action plan. Your action plan should include specific tasks that will need to be accomplished, complete with due dates and the names of the people to be held responsible.

Follow these steps to develop your detailed action plan:

1. Clarify your goal
   a) Ensure it is specific, measurable, attainable, relevant and timely
2. Build a list of tasks
   a) Write down all action steps that you may need to achieve the goal
   b) Write down the resources needed to complete the task
   c) Write down who will be responsible for each task
3. Organize your list into a plan
   a) Decide on the order of action steps
   b) Rearrange your actions and ideas into a sequential order
   c) Review this list and see if there are any ways to simplify it further
4. Anticipate problems and outline contingency plans

Describe your action plan for each of the goals you described in the previous section.

You've defined your target market and your products and services. You've developed your marketing and sales plan and your operations plan. You've described your company's leadership team and you have established written goals and developed action plans for achieving them. The next step is to figure out what it will cost, how you're going to pay for it, and how much profit you'll generate.

CHAPTER 10

FINANCIAL FORECASTS AND BUDGETS

"If you don't have regular and accurate financial statements, you're driving your business 100 miles an hour down a one-way street the wrong way, at night, in the fog, without lights."

—Jim Blasingame

Now that you have done your market research and analysis; identified your target market; defined your product and service; developed your marketing and sales plan, operations, and leadership and staffing plan; and set your goals and created your actions plan, it's time to work on your financial plan. The financial plan is a critical component of nearly all business plans. Running a successful business means paying close attention to how much money you are bringing in, and how much money you are spending. A good financial plan goes a long way to help determine when to hire new employees or buy a new piece of equipment. If you are a startup or are seeking funding, a solid financial plan helps you figure out how much capital your business needs to get started or to grow, so you know how much money to ask for from the bank or from investors.

This is often what small volume builders, remodelers, and trade contractors find most daunting, but it doesn't have to be as intimidating as it seems. Business financials are less complicated than you think, and a business degree is certainly not required to build a solid financial forecast.

The business financials you include in your business plan are "pro forma" financial statements. Pro forma financial statements are financial statements based on certain assumptions and projections. Your pro forma financial statements should include the following:

- Revenue Projections
  - Revenue or Sales
  - Cost of Goods Sold (COGS)
  - Gross Profit
- Work In Progress Projections
- Operating Expense Budget
- Income or Profit and Loss Statement
- Balance Sheet
- Cash Flow Statement
- Breakeven Analysis

I recommend that your revenue and operating expense budget projections include monthly projections for the first 2 years and annual projections for the remaining 3 to 5 years.

Following are brief overviews of the pro forma financial statements you should include in this section.

Revenue Projections

Your revenue projections include your projections for revenue or sales, cost of goods sold (COGS), and operating expenses.

Revenue or Sales

Your revenue projection should include rows projecting your revenue for each of your product types and services. Revenue and sales projections should include only revenue from completed projects or projects being done on a percentage complete basis.

If you are a builder, those rows might include the following:

3000–3490 Sales and Revenues 3050 Sales, developed lots
3110 Sales, single-family, production
3120 Sales, single-family, custom designed
3125 Sales, single–family, custom, no land
3190 Sales, other
3370 Design fees collected 3400 Miscellaneous income
3410 Interest income
3420 Dividend income
3450 Earned discounts

If you are a remodeler, those rows might include the following: 3000–3490 Sales and Revenues

3130 Sales, residential remodeling
3133 Sales, commercial and industrial remodeling 3135 Sales, insurance restoration
3137 Sales, repairs
3190 Sales, other
3370 Design fees collected 3400 Miscellaneous income
3410 Interest income
3420 Dividend income
3450 Earned discounts
3460 Earned rebates

Cost of Goods Sold (COGS)

Your revenue projection should also include corresponding rows projecting your cost of goods sold for each your product types or services. COGS includes only your direct costs – your hard cost of labor, materials, supplies, equipment, transportation, and other incidentals and services required to complete the project and your non-construction costs like architectural design, engineering, consulting, permitting, temporary utilities, and other costs.

If you are a builder, those rows would include the following:

3500–3790 Cost of Sales
3550 Cost of sales, developed lots
3610 Cost of sales, single-family, production
3620 Cost of sales, single-family, custom designed
3625 Cost of sales, single-family, custom, no land
3690 Cost of sales, other
3700 Direct construction costs for prior periods

If you are a remodeler, those rows might include the following:

3800–3899 Costs of Construction—Remodeling
3810 Direct labor
3820 Labor burden
3830 Building material
3840 Trade contractors
3850 Rental equipment
3860 Other direct construction costs
3870 Professional design fees

I strongly recommend using sub-accounts for each row corresponding with the various rows in your Sales and Revenue section. This will enable you to compare the revenue generated by each product or service type, i.e. Residential Remodeling, Commercial and Industrial Remodeling, Insurance Restoration, Repairs, etc. with the cost of goods sold for each product or service type to determine your gross margin percentage for each.

Cost of Goods should also include rows for indirect construction costs which are costs spread out over several jobs.

4000–4990 Indirect Construction Cost
4010 Superintendents
4020 Laborers
4030 Production managers
4040 Architects, drafters, estimators, purchasers
4110 Payroll taxes
4120 Workers' compensation insurance
4130 Health and accident insurance
4265 Mobile phones, pagers, radios, field
4410 Lease payments, construction vehicles
4420 Mileage reimbursement
4430 Repairs and maintenance, construction vehicles
4440 Operating expenses, construction vehicles
4450 Taxes, licenses, insurance, construction vehicles
4510 Rent, construction equipment
4530 Repairs and maintenance, construction equipment

4540 Operating expenses, construction equipment
4550 Taxes and insurance, construction equipment
4560 Small tools and supplies
4710 Salaries and wages, warranty 4720 Material, warranty
4730 Trade contractors, warranty

Gross Profit

Finally, your revenue projection should include your Gross Profit projection, i.e. your projected revenue minus your projected COGS.

Operating Expense Budget

Your operating expense budget projection is your projected financing expenses, sales and marketing expenses, and general and administrative expenses.

5000–5990 Financing Expenses
5000–5090 Interest
5100–5190 Construction Loan Points and Fees
5200–5290 Closing Costs

6000–6990 Sales and Marketing Expenses
6000–6090 Sales Salaries, Commissions
6100–6190 Payroll Taxes and Benefits, Sales and Marketing
6200–6290 Sales Office Expenses
6300–6390 Advertising and Sales Promotion
6400–6490 Sales Vehicles, Travel, and Entertainment
6600–6690 Model Home Maintenance
6700–6790 Sales and Marketing Fees
6800–6890 Depreciation
6900–6990 Other Marketing Expenses

8000–8990 General and Administrative Expense
8000–8090 Salaries and Wages
8100–8190 Payroll Taxes and Benefits
8200–8290 Office Expenses
8300–8390 Technology and Computer Expenses
8400–8490 Vehicles, Travel, and Entertainment
8500–8590 Taxes
8600–8690 Insurance
8700–8790 Professional Services
8800–8890 Depreciation Expenses
8900–8990 General and Administrative Expense, Other

9000–9990 Other Income and Expenses

9100–9190 Other Income
9200–9290 Other Expenses

Net Profit

Your net profit projection is simply your gross profit projection minus your operating expenses.

Work In Progress Projections

If you are a builder who builds spec homes or if you finance the construction of pre-sold homes, your pro forma financial statements should include work-in-progress projections. Like your revenue projections, your work in progress projection should include rows projecting your draws for each of the project types you are financing and corresponding rows projecting your cost of goods sold for each of those project types.

Income or Profit and Loss Statement

Your pro forma income or profit and loss statement (P&L) is an annual statement. The profit and loss statement pulls the annual totals from your revenue, cost of goods sold, and operating expense budget. In addition to the dollar totals, your profit & loss statement should show each of these numbers as a percentage of total sales.

Balance Sheet

Like your pro forma profit and loss statement, your pro forma balance sheet is an annual statement. The balance sheet provides an overview of the financial health of your business. It lists the assets in your company, the liabilities, and your (the owner's) equity. If you subtract the company's liabilities from assets, you can determine the net worth of the company. The assets include the value of your work in progress – an asset – and the amounts owed on the corresponding construction loans – liabilities.

Cash Flow Statement

Your pro forma cash flow statement is a monthly projection of the amount of cash (money in the bank) that you have at the end of each month. Your cash flow statement should start with the amount of cash you have on hand; add the amount of new cash received from customers on percent- age complete project, from draws against construction loans, and from other sources; and subtract cash paid out. This will leave you with your total available cash at the end of each month. (Starting cash + cash in – cash out = ending cash).

Your pro forma cash flow statement will show you when you might be low on cash, and when you might have available cash to invest in software or equipment. Your cash flow statement will help you to identify your low cash points and consider options to bring in additional cash. Above all, your cash flow statement will help you determine how much money you might need to borrow to sustain or grow your company.

Appendix C provides examples of pro forma financial statement worksheets and instructions for downloading the Microsoft® Excel® workbook containing the actual worksheets that you can fill in and use to complete your pro forma financial statements.

Break-even Analysis

The break-even analysis tells you what you need to sell and produce (earn) to reach that point when your business has earned enough to pay all its operating costs and expenses but has not yet earned enough to make a profit. Determining a break-even point requires knowledge of your fixed and variable overhead costs, the cost of goods sold and the selling price of your services. Remember, total operating costs and expenses are the sum of: owners' compensation; financing costs; sales and marketing costs; and general and administrative expense (G&A). The simple break-even point is when:

Overhead$ = Gross profit$

Pro Forma Assumptions

Your Financial Forecasts and Budgets section of your business plan should detail the key assumptions upon which your projections are based. Examples of key assumptions are the number of qualified leads generated, the closing ratio, the number of sales, and the average project value.

Knowing what your assumptions are as you start a business can make the difference between business success and business failure. When you recognize your assumptions, you can set out to prove that your assumptions are correct. The more that you can minimize your assumptions, the more likely it is that your business will succeed.

Key Ratios

Financial ratios identify relationships among the different items in financial statements. Calculating ratios is a popular method of analyzing financial statements and is used to pinpoint where a company is doing well or where it needs to improve. A ratio is calculated by dividing one item on a financial statement by another item; the ratio shows the relationship between the two items. Information from the income statement and balance sheet can be used to check the ability of the company to pay its financial obligations, determine trends, and compare results with industry trends and business goals.

Ratios are commonly classified as:

- Liquidity ratios
- Profitability ratios
- Return on investment ratios
- Leverage ratios

Liquidity ratios reflect a business's capability to meet current debt obligations. Leverage ratios reflect how effectively the business uses certain fixed costs to enhance returns on investments. These comparisons help determine the business's financial strength and efficiency.

Small volume builders and remodelers should strive to achieve and maintain the following Financial and Operating Ratios:

Current Ratio or Working Capital Ratio – 1.2 to 1.4

The current ratio or working capital ratio is current assets divided by current liabilities.

Current Ratio = Current Assets ÷ Current Liabilities

Because it is expressed as a ratio, it is size blind, so you can tell if it is an appropriate number for any sized business. A current ratio below 1 means that the company's current debt obligations exceed the amount of current assets the company has on hand to pay them. The company is operating with negative working capital. A general rule of thumb is that a current ratio between 1.5 and 2.0 of current assets for every dollar of current liability is acceptable, A current ratio less than 1.0 is an impending problem, (i.e., trouble is less than a year away). Remodelers, custom builders and those without land, buildings and other more difficult assets to liquidate, can fall into the 1.2 - 1.4 range.

Quick Ratio or Acid-Test Ratio

The quick ratio, or acid-test ratio, is a more conservative version of the current ratio. It compares highly liquid assets such as cash and accounts receivable against current liabilities. It does not take into account current assets that would be more difficult to convert to cash, such as work in progress that has not been billed. This ratio tells a company how well it can meet its current obligations immediately, i.e. within days. Normally the ratio should be no less than 1.0.

Quick Ratio = Cash + Marketable Securities + Accounts Receivable ÷ Current liabilities

Working Capital to Sales Ratio

The working capital to sales ratio is an example of a leverage ratio and is useful for calculating the approximate amount of working capital a business needs, given a sales projection. The ratio is calculated by subtracting the current liabilities from the current assets found on the balance sheet. This gives you working capital, which is then compared to total sales found on the income statement.

Current Assets – Current Liabilities = Working Capital Working
Capital to Sales Ratio = Working Capital ÷ Total Sales

The amount of working capital needed depends on the rate at which homes or remodel projects are completed. The longer a spec home, new home or remodeling project takes to close, the greater the percentage of working capital needed.

Debt to Equity Ratio (Leverage) - 2 to 1

The Debt to Equity Ratio measures how much money a company can safely borrow over long periods of time by measuring the money owed to creditors in relation to the company's equity value, i.e. retained earnings and invested capital from previous years plus the current year's profit and loss. It is calculated by taking the company's total short-term and long-term debts (or liabilities) and dividing that number by the owner's equity.

Debt to Equity Ratio = Total Liabilities ÷ Owner's Equity

The higher the leverage a company has, the higher the risk of failure. This is because as the debt/equity ratio increases, interest takes more and more of the earnings, leaving less for profits and less of a margin for poor performance. Tracking this ratio tells the owner when he is going to lose the confidence of his banker or investors. That number is generally over 4-to-1. Said differently, it is when outsiders own 80 percent of the company and you only own 20 percent.

When the above ratios start faltering there are things you should do:

- Raise prices.
- Cut construction costs (COGS).
- Cut overhead expenditures; make do with what you have.
- Sell off poorly performing assets, particularly long-term assets such as land.
- Turn short-term line of credit financing into long-term financing with lower fixed rates and collateral if necessary; this lowers annual cash payments.
- Turn cash faster, bill at the start of phases, enforce interest owed on late bills, always take your discounts, (it is like 72 percent annual interest!). Do what it takes to collect from slow paying or overly demanding clients

Owner's Salary as a Percentage of Sales

This ratio would most likely be classified as a profitability ratio since the owner decides to either make more net profit or sacrifice net profit for greater owner's compensation. How does your business compare with others in the industry? As the owner, are you overpaying or underpaying yourself? Once you have calculated this ratio by dividing your annual sales revenue into your annual salary, you can compare this ratio to others in your industry.

Owner's Salary as a % of Sales = Owner's Annual Salary ÷ Annual Sales Revenue

For smaller remodelers, 10% of sales is a good target for salary with benefits, so adjust your pay package accordingly before comparing. Once you reach over two million dollars in sales, the percentage is gradually reduced until you are around 5% for 10 million dollars and up. Builders usually take less than these percentages, but numbers less than 7% would be considered underpaid except for very large production builders.

Financial Analysis and Conclusions

This section includes conclusions you want drawn to the attention of anyone reading this document.

Capital Requirements

What are your capital requirements, if any, over the next 1 to 5 years?

Use of Funds Statement

If you are raising money from bankers or investors, you should include a brief section plan that details exactly how you plan on using their cash. You don't need to go into excruciating detail about how every dollar will be spent. Just describe the major areas where the funds will be used, such as building and maintaining a model or model homes, building and maintaining a sales center or showroom, purchasing equipment, etc.

If you're looking for an investor, specify the percent of equity ownership offered in return.

Exit Strategy

The last thing that you might need to include in your Financial Plan chapter is a section on your exit strategy. An exit strategy is your plan for eventually selling your business, either to another company or to the public in an IPO. If you have investors, they will want to know your thoughts on this. After all, your investors will want a return on their investment, and the only way they will get this is if the company is sold to someone else.

You've defined your target market and your products and services. You've developed your marketing and sales plan and your operations plan. You've described your company's leadership team and you have established written goals and developed action plans for achieving them. You've created your pro forma financial statements. The next step is to craft your company vision statement, mission statement, and unique selling proposition.

CHAPTER 11

VISION, MISSION, CORE VALUES AND UNIQUE SELLING PROPOSITION

"Your ability to prosper as a company is not about what you sell, it's about what you believe."

—Simon Sinek, author of "Start With Why"

Vision Statement

A vision statement creates a picture, in words, of future success that challenges, guides and inspires a group to achieve its mission. A vision statement should be brief, simple, appropriate and challenging, with a long-term horizon. As the late Stephen R. Covey was known for saying, "Begin with the end in mind." One of the more famous vision statements is attributed to President John F. Kennedy: "By the end of the decade, we will put a man on the moon." The statement was powerful and effective because it created a strong visual image and was easily understood by everyone who heard it.

Susan Ward on About.com provides the following definition:

> "A vision statement is sometimes called a picture of your company in the future but it's so much more than that. Your vision statement is your inspiration, the framework for all your strategic planning.
>
> "A vision statement may apply to an entire company or to a single division of that company. Whether for all or part of an organization, the vision statement answers the question, 'Where do we want to go?'
>
> "What you are doing when creating a vision statement is articulating your dreams and hopes for your business. It reminds you of what you are trying to build.
>
> "While a vision statement doesn't tell you how you're going to get there, it does set the direction for your business planning."

Mission Statement

A mission statement describes the type of business and its purpose as it exists today. It may also include values and beliefs that help define its culture and its brand. It answers the questions,

"Why do we exist? What makes us different, unique?" As you craft your mission statement, remember it is usually an internal device as well as a public statement.

David Packard, the co-founder of Hewlett-Packard said, "People assume, wrongly, that a company exists simply to make money. While this is an important result of a company's existence, we must go deeper and find the real reasons for our being. Purpose which should last 100 years should not be confused with specific goals or business strategies which should change many times in 100 years."

In today's marketplace, builders and general contractors struggle to keep their heads above water, operating in a constant sea of change, intense competition, and rising consumer expectations. Yet, there is one constant they can rely on: their purpose. In staying connected and committed to this purpose, they can accomplish what many businesses fail to do – sustain growth.

In his best seller, "Built To Last," Jim Collins writes, "Leaders die, products become obsolete, markets change, new technologies emerge, and management fads come and go, but core ideology in a great company endures as a source of guidance and inspiration."

Whether you're working to discover a new purpose, or already have one in place, it's useful to consider these questions to ensure you're on the right track and utilizing the full benefits of your purpose.

- Is it authentic and inspiring?
- Do your employees know it and believe in it?
- Does it align with every decision you make at every level of your organization?
- Is it communicated to your customers by your actions?
- Do your customers and others outside of your organization know your purpose?
- Do you believe in it?

Your mission statement should be:

Short. It should be no more than one page.

Clear. Precise in the message it conveys, easy to understand and remember.

Forward thinking. It should express where you want to go, not just where you are. It should capture the essence of what you want to achieve.

Personal. It is your values and beliefs and how you do business. Avoid generic statements. (Who doesn't build a "quality" home?)

Meaningful. The mission statement is the keystone that the entire business planning process is built around. The vision and mission statement should guide the daily activities of every person involved in the business. If it doesn't mean something to you, it is meaningless.

Lofty yet attainable. If it is too idealistic or impossible to achieve, it will be difficult to convey real meaning. It is not a marketing statement.

Don't fall into the trap of spending too much time on your mission statement. You'll end up with a long, generic statement about how your company is serving its customers, employees, etc. Your company mission should encompass, at a very high level, what you are trying to do. Frankly, your mission statement and your overall value proposition might even be the same thing.

Once you create your mission statement, review it every few years to make sure that it is still relevant to the work you are doing, and that it continues to communicate your

Who are we and what do we do (in 15 seconds or less)?

What methods and values do we employ and apply to do what we do? What specific outcomes do we want to create through our efforts?

How do we measure our success?

Core Values

Core values are the fundamental beliefs of a company. For builders and remodelers, the core values of the company often reflect the owner's fundamental beliefs. The core values are the guiding principles that dictate behavior and action. Core values can help employees to know what is right from wrong and help companies to determine if they are on the right path and fulfilling their business goals. Core values create an unwavering and unchanging guide. There are many different types of core values and many different examples of core values depending upon the context.

There are countless types of core values, as you can see, so you will need to choose the ones that are right for you or your organization.

Here are some examples of core values: Dependable

Reliable
Loyal
Committed
Open-minded
Consistent
Honest
Efficient
Innovative
Creative
Motivated
Positive
Passionate
Respectful
Respected

While you include your company's core values in your business plan, the best way to identify these values is to observe how you and your employees act and behave. A core value is only a true core value if it has an active influence and if you and your employees manage to live by it, at least most of the time.

List the company's core values

Unique Selling Proposition

Your unique selling proposition, or USP, is what separates your business from your competitors. It defines your unique position within the marketplace and gives you an edge over other businesses.

Why is a unique selling proposition important?

Every competitor in your field is vying for attention. From marketing plans to advertisements, consumers hear a lot of noise. To cut through this clutter, and turn your target audience into loyal customers, you need a value proposition.

In a crowded marketplace, you need a unique selling proposition to compete. That's probably the biggest reason why a unique selling proposition is vital to your business.

Whatever your value proposition is, it must be something that the competition can't claim, or at the very least something they don't use as a marketing tool.

How do you create a unique selling proposition?

One of the best ways to create a successful selling proposition is to make a connection with your audience that pushes them to act.

Finding a unique selling proposition takes some time and legwork. It's more than whipping up a clever tagline. To create a unique selling proposition, you must know your customer and your business. Plus, you must understand how your product or service fits into our consumer-driven world.

And that's just a start. I'm not saying this to scare you - rather to express how in-depth the process is.

"It's not about shouting louder. It's about marketing smarter. Creating compelling messages that connect with consumers, engage their hearts (not just their minds), and turn them into loyal brand ambassadors who will help you get the word out and build your brand," says Julie Cottineau, the former Vice President of Brand for Virgin, and current owner of a brand consultancy BrandTwist.

What is it that our customers need – not want – that they are having difficulty receiving and obtaining and which our company, better than any other, can provide.

What specific customer need are we going to fulfill?

How will we overcome or control the obstacles and challenges that exist within the market and the industry?

What will be our competitive advantage?

What sets your business apart? The answer to that question usually leads entrepreneurs to define their unique selling proposition, or USP.

Here are some tips to help you create a unique selling proposition.

Don't Try to Appeal to Everyone

Your unique selling proposition isn't meant to appeal to everyone. You want a well-defined audience. Refer to your buyer persona you created from your market research.

As Lisa Furgison noted in her Bplan.com article "How to Create a Unique Value Proposition, ""The biggest mistake businesses make is casting too wide a net, for fear of leaving anyone out. Women 25-54 is not a valid target segment, it's a census box." If you try to appeal to everyone, your business and product will get lost in the noise. "Don't be afraid to alienate a few people along the way. Brands that target everyone, connect with no one," says Julie Cottineau.

On the contrary—you want a value proposition that is attractive and effective to your target market. This will help you advertise and market your business alongside competitors while carving out a market share all your own.

Differentiate Yourself From The Pack

"In my practice, I think of a USP as a twist. Something unique, unexpected, and meaningful that can set you apart from the pack," she explains. "A USP is any aspect of your brand or business that is different from your competition and can be communicated to your audience to encourage people to try your brand or switch from another brand." says Julie Cottineau.

Whatever your value proposition is, it must be something that the competition can't claim, or at the very least something they don't use as a marketing tool.

Define the needs your product or business meets

Simply having the best product or the best customer service in the market isn't enough differentiation. Remember, every business thinks they have the best product. Take some time to figure out how your product meets the needs of your target market in a way that others can't.

Write down how your business or product can help others. Can your product do something that other products can't? List and cross off any need that your competitors can claim too.

Dispel Myths

Can your business or product dispel any myths or stereotypes? If your business or product is "going against the norm" in any way, or breaks commonly held myths, you can use that as leverage.

Create A Clear Mission And Message

A unique selling proposition goes deeper than a marketing plan; it should connect with your brand's mission. Does your mission overlap or coincide with the list of things that sets your business apart? Now you're starting to hone in on your value proposition.

Make a list of possible value propositions that fit your business. Again, this isn't going to be something you whip up in 20 minutes. Write a few down, stew on them for a bit, and refine them. You want a clear message.

Using your list of unique attributes and your brand's mission, you can start to mold that information into a clear message. Rework it until you have one succinct sentence that will become your value proposition.

Bring It To Life

Once you've defined your value proposition, you must bring it to life. In other words, you need to turn it into a marketing tool. From slogans, your website design, your social media pages, your collateral material, your value proposition should seep into every aspect of your business.

You can't create a value proposition alone in your basement, either. You must test it. Run it by a small group of your target market to ensure your value proposition resonates with customers you're trying to reach.

Creating a value proposition is time consuming, but certainly to your advantage in the long term.

Now that you've crafted your vision and mission statements and your unique selling proposition, you've completed all the elements of your internal business plan. If you want to continue, the next step is to describe your company.

CHAPTER 12

THE FINAL STEP - THE REVIEW PLAN

"However beautiful the strategy, you should occasionally look at the results."

—Winston Churchill

You've probably heard the saying "The best laid plans of mice and men often go awry." A real business plan is always wrong — hence the regular review and revisions — and never done, because the process of review and revise is vital. The best planning is iterative; it's kept alive and it adapts.

Many small businesses fail because of fundamental shortcomings in their business planning. Your business plan must be realistic and, most importantly, based on accurate, current information and educated projections for the future.

Just writing a business plan does not guarantee your success. The best way to extract value from your business plan is to use it as an ongoing management tool. To do this, your business plan must be constantly revisited and revised to reflect current conditions and the new information that you've collected as you run your business.

When you're running a business, you are learning new things every day: what your customers like, what they don't like, which marketing strategies work, which ones don't. Your business plan should reflect those learnings to guide your future strategy.

Build a plan, but don't just stick it in a drawer. Track your performance as you go so you can see if you're reaching your goals. Your plan will help you discover what's working so you can build your business.

Having a plan and updating it regularly means that you are tracking your performance and adjusting as you go. If things aren't working, you know it. And, if things are going well, you know what to do more of.

It's a tool that you use to refine and adapt your strategy as you go, continuing to understand your market as it changes and refining your business to the ever-changing needs of your customers. As Robert Fulghum suggests, "If at first you don't succeed, redefine success."

To effectively leverage your business plan, view it as a growth engine. I recommend that you schedule a monthly review. The review doesn't have to take longer than an hour, but it needs to be a regular, recurring meeting on your calendar. In your monthly review, go over your key numbers compared to your plan, review the milestones you planned to accomplish, set new milestones, and do a quick review of your overall strategy

Here are some tips to extract the most value from your plan in the least amount of time:

- The markets are constantly changing. Continually monitor the market for these changes and modify your plan accordingly.

- Keep your sales forecast and expense budget current. As you learn more about customer buying patterns, revise your forecast.
- Compare your planned budgets and forecasts with your actual results monthly and adjust your plan based on the results.
- Take immediate corrective action when you begin to deviate from plan benchmarks, goals, and objectives.
- Follow-up with an annual plan review and update: Drop off the preceding year; roll in a new 3rd or 5th year, with full forecasts, goals and operating budgets.

Now you've completed all essential elements of your internal business plan. The next two chapters describe the remaining two elements required for an external business plan: the company overview and the executive summary.

CHAPTER 13

COMPANY OVERVIEW

The company overview will most likely be the shortest section of your business plan. As noted previously, if your business plan is for internal use only, this section can be omitted. For external plans, this section is a summary of the company's legal structure, ownership, history, and location.

Legal Structure and Ownership

The company overview section of your business plan should include a description of your company's current legal structure and ownership. Lenders and potential investors will want to know the structure of the business and who the owners are before they will consider lending money or investing.

Is you company a C-corporation? An S-corporation? A limited liability company? A partnership? A sole proprietorship? Where is your company registered? If a corporation, who are the share- holders, and what are their respective percentage of ownership? If a limited liability company who are the members and what are their respective percentage of ownership? If a partnership, who are the partners and what are their respective percentage of ownership? If a sole proprietorship, who is/ are the owner(s)?

Company History

If you are writing a business plan for an existing company, this section should include a brief history of the company and highlight major historical achievements. When was the company founded? Again, keep this section short — no more than a few paragraphs at most.

This section is especially useful to give context to the rest of your plan and can also be very use- ful for internal plans. The company history section can provide new employees with background on the company, so they have a better context for the work that they are doing and where the company has come from over the years.

Location

This section should also describe your company's current business location and any facilities that the company owns.

Construction Operations

This section should also describe the geographic area(s) in which you operate, i.e. cities, counties, other jurisdictions

Affiliations

This section should also list the professional and civic organizations your company is affiliated with. These would include local and state HBA's, the National Association of Home Builders, the National Association of Realtors, the Chamber of Commerce, the Better Business Bureau, etc.

Outside Support

Finally, this section should include information on your company's outside professional support and advisors. These would include your accountant, insurance agent, banker, attorney, etc.

If you are a member of the National Association of Home Builders, I highly recommend that you consider joining a 20 Club. Innovative and ambitious home builders and remodelers have been taking advantage of 20 Clubs, a unique networking program, for more than 16 years. The 20 Clubs are comprised of builders and remodelers from non-competing markets who meet several times a year to share their wisdom and learn ways to improve operations and increase bottom lines from each other. Members share and compare financial information, look for trouble spots, and offer each other advice on how to increase their profit ratios and improve their performance. Visit nahb.org and search for "20 Clubs" or email 20clubs@nahb.org for more information.

The next section of your business plan is the Executive Summary.

CHAPTER 14

EXECUTIVE SUMMARY

"You never get a second chance to make a first impression."

—Andrew Grant

The executive summary is your business's calling card. It needs to be succinct and hit the key highlights of the plan. The executive summary introduces your company, explains what you do, and lays out what you're looking for from your readers.

Structurally, the executive summary is the first chapter of your business plan. And while it's the first thing that people will read, I recommend writing it after everything else is done, so you know exactly what appears in the rest of your business plan and will be better prepared to write it.

If you are writing an internal business plan, you can skip the executive summary or greatly reduce it in scope. If you choose to write an executive summary for an internal plan, treat the executive summary as an overview of the strategic direction of the company, to ensure that all team members are on the same page. Make the purpose of the plan clear, and make sure the highlights are covered, but you don't necessarily need to repeat the business location, your product or service description, the details about the management team, and funding requirements.

If you are writing a standard business plan, the executive summary is a critical component of your business plan. Make it as clear and concise as possible. Introduce your company and cover the key highlights of your business without going into too much detail.

Ideally, the executive summary can act as a stand-alone document that covers the highlights of your detailed plan. The purpose of writing an executive summary is also to deliver a hard sell if you're shopping around for capital.

Investors and lenders these days expect a concise, focused plan. Many potential investors will never make it beyond the executive summary. In fact, it's very common for investors to ask for only the executive summary when they are evaluating your business. That's why it should be designed to be a quick read that sparks interest and makes your investors feel eager to hear more. It needs to be compelling and intriguing. Make your prospective investor want to keep reading. Convince them to invest in your business. After looking over your executive summary, your target reader is either going to throw your business plan away or, if they like what they read, they'll often follow up with a request for a complete plan, a pitch presentation, and other data about your business.

Opinions differ on how long an executive summary should be. Some insist that it should be limited to a page or two. Others recommend a more detailed summary, taking as much as 10 pages, covering enough information to substitute for the plan itself. I recommend that your standard executive summary format be about a page of writing, followed by easy-to-skim subsections that highlight your main points. These subsections should include:

- Company Information
- Financial Performance and Forecasts
- Goals
- Capital Requirements
- Leadership Team
- Market Analysis
  - Target Market
  - Competition
- Product and Service Strategy
- Marketing and Sales Strategy
- Risks

At the top of the page, right under your business name, include your unique selling proposition. For a standard business plan, the first paragraph of your executive summary should generally include your company's name, background, current situation, and legal structure i.e. C-Corp, S-Corp, LLC, sole proprietorship, its location, and a brief description of your product, i.e. entry- level homes, move-up homes, design-build custom homes, remodeling, etc. and the purpose of your plan. It should introduce you, your business, and your product.

Financial Performance and Forecasts: This first sub-section should provide a summary of your company's financial performance and forecasts. If your company has been in existence for some time, provide a chart like the one below showing your historical financial performance.

Historical Financial Performance										
Description	**Year 1**		**Year 2**		**Year 3**		**Year 4**		**Year 5**	
	$	**%**	**$**	**%**	**$**	**%**	**$**	**%**	**$**	**%**
Revenue										
Cost of Goods Sold										
Gross Profit										
Operating Expense										
Net Profit										
Notes:										

Market Analysis: This subsection should summarize your market analysis. Briefly summarize your analysis of national and local industry and economic conditions. Briefly summarize your analysis of market segmentation, niche markets, and submarkets.

Target Market: Copy your Buyer Persona from the Market Research and Analysis section of your business plan and provide specific details on the market size.

Competition: Summarize the Main Competitors subsection of the Market Research and Analysis section of your business plan. Identify your top competitors and briefly discuss their strengths, weaknesses, and vulnerabilities as they exist today. Briefly discuss the barriers to entry and the available opportunities. Briefly discuss the risks you identified.

Product and Service Strategy: In this subsection, briefly describe the products and services offered, the problem they are solving, or the need you are filling for your target market. Also, briefly describe any new products or services you intend to bring to the market over the next one to five years.

Marketing and Sales Strategy: In this subsection, summarize your marketing and sales strategy as described in detail in the Marketing and Sales Plan section of your business plan.

Describe your brand. Describe your sales objectives, sales plans and strategies as they address the performance forecasts for the plan. Describe briefly your current sales staff, sales training, and sales development processes.

Risks: In this final subsection, summarize the top business risks facing your company today as described in detail in the Market Research and Analysis section of your business.

Congratulations! You've finished writing your business plan. The last step is to assemble the supporting documents.

CHAPTER 15

SUPPORTING DATA APPENDIX

The Supporting Data Appendix is the place to include all pertinent supporting documents. The reason for creating this section is to back up what you have stated in your business plan by providing the full documents. It allows the main body of the plan to read as a cohesive document that focuses on each aspect of your business without getting bogged down with numbers and implicit details.

I've tried to include recommendations on exhibits to include throughout the text of the various sections of your business. However, I recommend that you reread your business plan to see if you have referred to any specific studies or surveys, or made comparisons. All copies of documents should be legible and complete.

There are specific documents that lenders might want to see. These could vary according to your business and the stage of your business development. The following are recommendations of documents the builder or remodeler should include:

Company Overview Exhibits

- Copy of your registration as a corporation, LLC, partnership, or sole proprietorship
- Copy of your Contractor License or Registration
- Copies of your membership certificates in local and trade associations
- Copies of information on professionals who support your company
- A list of your past customers
- A list of your business references

Market Research and Analysis Exhibits

- Copies of marketing research studies and other documents used

Product and Services Plan Exhibits

- Copies of your Standard Floor Plans
- Copies of documents that describe your products and services

Marketing and Sales Plan Exhibits

- Copy of your website
- Copies of your social media pages
- Copy of your e-newsletter
- Copies of your eBooks and white papers
- Copies of your newspaper advertising.
- Copies of your brochures, postcards, catalogues
- Examples of your email marketing
- Copies of your collateral material
- Sample Sales Agreement
- Sample Warranty

Operations Plan Exhibits

- Copy of your Company Chart of Accounts
- Copy of a Sample Job Cost Report
- Copy of your Trade Contract, Work Order, and Purchase Order
- Copy of your Pre-Construction Conference Agenda
- Copy of a Sample Project Schedule
- Copies of your Quality Control Checklists
- Copy of Sample Red Tag

Leadership Team and Staffing Exhibits

- Resumes of Leadership Team Members
- Copy of your Company Organizational Chart

Financial Forecasts and Budgets Exhibits

Lenders and potential investors are going to expect your business plan to contain copies of your:

- Pro Forma Revenue Projections
- Pro Forma Work in Progress Projections
- Pro Forma Operating Expense Budget
- Pro Forma Income or Profit and Loss Statement
- Pro Forma Balance Sheet
- Pro Forma Cash Flow Statement
- Breakeven Analysis

END NOTES

1. Brinckmann, J., Grichnik, D., & Kapsa, D. (2010). Should entrepreneurs plan or just storm the castle? A meta-analysis on contextual factors impacting the business planning–performance relationship in small firms. Journal of Business Venturing, 25(1), 24-40. doi: 10.1016/j.jbusvent.2008.10.007
2. Burke, A., Fraser, S., & Greene, F. J. (2010). The multiple effects of business planning on new venture performance. *Journal of Management Studies,* 47(3), 391-415.
3. Upton, N., Teal, E. J., & Felan, J. T. (2001). Strategic and business planning practices of fast growth family firms. Journal of Small Business Management, 39(1), 60-72.a

HAVE CHUCK SPEAK AT YOUR NEXT EVENT

LOOKING FOR A PROFESSIONAL SPEAKER for your next event? Chuck Miller is the answer.

Inspirational, fun, and relevant, Chuck Miller is a business planning keynote speaker, author, and strategist who works with builders, remodelers, and other construction-related companies want- ing to control their business - instead of letting it control them. Chuck isn't just another self-proclaimed business planning keynote speaker; he has almost fifty years of experience managing construction companies and their projects. He has been involved in the planning and construction of over 3,000 single and multi-family homes; mixed-use buildings; commercial buildings including medical and dental offices, business offices, hotels, and recreational facilities; and institutional buildings including a medium-security prison.

Chuck is the founder of Chuck Miller Consulting LLC. He understands the special needs of small-volume builders and remodelers and works with them to create custom solutions. Small businesses in the construction industry have the second highest 5-year failure rate of all industries. Chuck Miller Consulting was formed to help small businesses in the construction industry survive and thrive beyond 5 years and to increase the five year survival rate for small businesses in the construction industry. Chuck Miller Consulting provides business management, training, consulting, and coaching to small volume builders and remodelers and construction related companies. Chuck also provides arbitration and mediation services and expert witness service on construction businessrelated issues.

Chuck is also founder and Chief Education Officer of Chuck Miller Education Services LLC, a residential home building, remodeling, and new home sales training company whose goal is to foster success in the industry. He has been an instructor for NAHB since 1999 and is one of NAHB's Master Instructors.

Chuck was also founder, President and CEO of Chuck Miller Construction Inc., a nationally-recognized design-build custom home builder and remodeler located in Boise, Idaho.

Chuck has spoken to audiences ranging in size from ten to hundreds at local and national industry events like the International Builders Show.

Book Chuck for your next event and treat your audience to an informative and educational program packed with practical information.

Connect with Chuck

www.chuckmillerconsulting.com

ChuckMillerEducation.com

Twitter: @boisebuilder

Facebook.com/ChuckMillerConsulting

Facebook.com/ChuckMillerEducationServices

Linkedin.com/in/chuckmiller-consultant-coach-arbitrator-expert-witness-author

APPENDIX A

ADDITIONAL RESOURCES

National Association of Home Builders courses:

Business Management for Building Professionals
Business Accounting and Job Cost
Construction Contracts and Law
Design/Build
Customer Service
Financial Management
Profitable Business Through Quality Practices
Risk Management and Insurance for Building Professionals
Diversification: Capitalizing on New Business Opportunities
Basics of Building
Project Management
Home Technology Integration
Land Acquisition & Development Financing
Land Development: Site Planning & Zoning
Marketing & Communication Strategies for Aging & Accessibility (CAPS I)
Design/Build Solutions for Aging & Accessibility (CAPS II)
Universal Design/Build
Green Building for Building Professionals
Advanced Green Building: Project Management
Advanced Green Building: Building Science
Marketing & Sales for Building Professionals
Certified New Home Sales Professional (CSP)
    CSP I: The Art and Science of Selling
    CSP II: Understanding New Home Construction
    CSP III: Selling Skills for New Home Sales Professional
House Construction as a Selling Tool

Programs and White Papers:
"Where Does Profit Really Come From?" – The Aspire Institute www.theaspireinstitute.com

"Why Contractors Take Bad Jobs" - The Aspire Institute https://.theaspireinstitute.com/why- contractors-take-bad-jobs

"Beating the Boom & Bust Business Cycles for the Construction Industry" – The Aspire Institute https://theaspireinstitute.com/beating-the-cycle-landing-page/

Books:

Accounting & Financial Management for Residential Construction, 5th Edition by Emma Shinn

The Cost of Doing Business Study, 2022 Edition

Remodelers' Cost of Doing Business Study, 2020 Edition

Managing Your Business with 7 Key Numbers by Jeffrey Kenneth Prager and Scott Stroud

Internet Marketing: The Key to Increased Home Sales by Mitch Levinson, MIRM, CSP

Social Media 3.0: It's Easier Than You Think by Carol L. Morgan, MIRM, CAPS, CSP

Build a Successful Sales Program by Perry Goldman

From Good Market Research to Great Marketing: A How-to Guide for Home Builders by Colleen Edwards

Sales & Marketing Checklists for Profit-Driven Home Builders by Jan Mitchell

FANtastic Marketing: Leverage Your Fan Factor, Build a Blockbuster Brand, Score New Customers, and Wipe Out the Competition by Meredith Oliver

FANtastic Selling: The 10 Undeniable Traits of Rock-Star, Top-Producing, Quota-Busting Salespeople by Meredith Oliver

Master What Matters ... How to Create New Home Marketing That Guarantees Increased Traffic by Brian Flook MIRM and Shirley Mozingo

Financial Management for the Non-financial Manager: Take the Mystery Out of Running Your Homebuilding Business by Mike Benshoof

APPENDIX B

NAHB CHART OF ACCOUNTS (W/DESCRIPTIONS)

1000–1990 Assets

1000–1090 Cash

1010 Petty cash—All of a company's petty cash accounts, whether maintained in office or by construction superintendent in the field

1020 Cash on deposit, general—Demand deposits in bank for all regular trade receipts and disbursements

1030 Cash on deposit, payroll—Demand deposits in bank for payroll disbursements only (Generally, companies that employ their own crews and write a large number of payroll checks maintain a separate checking account to cover payroll. For each pay period, a check for the total amount of the payroll is written against the general account and deposited into the payroll account.)

1040 Cash on deposit, savings and money market—Deposits in savings and money market accounts

1050 Cash on deposit, held in escrow—Cash held at title companies, disbursing agents, and financial institutions, representing refundable customer deposits, completion escrows, or other escrowed funds

1060 Cash on deposit, operating reserve—Deposits in a dedicated savings or money market account set aside to stabilize the company's finances by providing a cushion against unexpected events, losses of income, and large unbudgeted expenses.

1100–1190 Short-term Investments

1110 Certificates of deposit—Funds deposited in interest-bearing certificates of deposit (CDs), maturing in less than one year

1120 Marketable securities—Funds invested in readily marketable stock of unaffiliated companies that management intends to dispose of within one year (In accordance with generally accepted accounting principles [GAAP], these investments should be carried at the lower of aggregate cost or market value. To adjust, credit this account and debit 2940, unrealized holding loss.)

1130 Government securities—Funds invested in securities issued by federal, state, or local authorities maturing in less than one year

1190 Other short-term investments—Funds invested in other instruments for set periods (usually less than one year) that earn interest or dividend income

1200–1290 Receivables

1210 Accounts receivable, trade—Amounts due to the business for construction, including customers' orders for extras, management services, or other services performed on open account

1220 Accounts receivable, other—Amounts due to the business for services not otherwise classified

1230 Notes receivable—Unpaid balances due to the company on notes received in full or partial settlement of open or short-term accounts

1250 Mortgage notes receivable, current year—Mortgages taken from purchasers in lieu of cash; payments due within 12 months

1260 Due on construction and development loans—Amounts due from financial institutions on construction and development loans (The balance of this account represents the amount of cash available from construction and development loans. When a loan is approved, debit this account to show how much cash is available through the loan, and credit 2220, acquisitions and development loans payable, or 2230, construction loans payable. As you draw cash from the loan, you decrease, or credit, 1260, due on construction and development loans, to show how much cash is available to draw from the loan. Alternatively, you can record draws against construction loans directly to account 2220, acquisitions and development loans payable, or 2230, construction loans payable.) 1265 Costs in excess of billings—Primarily used by remodelers, custom builders, and commercial builders to record costs that exceed their estimated costs (sometimes referred to as under billing) based upon the percentage of completion method

1270 Accrued interest receivable—Interest earned but not received from all sources such as bonds, notes, and mortgages

1280 Allowance for doubtful accounts—A contra account that has a credit balance reflecting the potential uncollectible amounts of any account in the receivables classification (A contra account reduces the balance of an account in this case, accounts receivable without changing the account itself.)

1290 Retentions (retainage) receivable—Amounts withheld by customers on progress billings. (When retentions become due, debit 1220, accounts receivable other, and credit 1290, retention receivable.)

1300–1390 Inventories

1310 Construction materials inventory—Control account for book value of construction materials purchased and stored, rather than delivered directly to a job in progress (As materials are allocated to a specific job, the cost is transferred and debited to 1430, direct construction cost, and credited to 1310, construction materials inventory. Excess materials purchased directly for a specific job and originally debited to 1430 should be debited to 1310 and credited to 1430 if the materials are transferred to inventory. Or they should be added to the cost of the house for which the materials are used.)

1320 Land held for development—Control account for cost of land purchased for future development (The cost of land increases by recording fees, legal fees, and other acquisition costs. Debit cost of land to 1410, land and land development, at the time the land is to be developed, and credit 1320, land held for development.)

1330 Property held for remodeling—Acquisition costs for properties held for future improvement or remodeling (Once the work is completed, they may be sold or held for investment.)

1400–1490 Work in Progress

1410 Land and land development—Control account for all land and land development costs. Cumulative cost of land and land development, including cost of raw land, financing and interest, land planning, engineering, grading, streets, curbs and gutters, sidewalks, storm sewers, temporary utilities, professional fees, permits, and other costs pertaining to the development of the raw land. (Refer to the Land Development Costs Subsidiary Ledger for subsidiary accounts detail.)

1412 Accumulated allocations, land, and land development costs—Accumulated write- offs to developed lots or to cost of sales for land and land development costs (At the time of closing, debit the cost of the lot to the appropriate cost of sales account in the 3500 to 3700 series and credit 1412.)

1420 Developed lots—Cost of lots developed prior to purchase to be used for construction (When a house is closed, debit the cost to the appropriate cost of sales account in the 3500 to 3700 series.)

1425 Reserve for impairment on developed lots—Reserve to reflect lower of cost or market value of developed lots

1430 Direct construction cost—Control account for all direct construction costs including permits, direct labor, materials, trade contractors, equipment rentals and any other direct charge to the units under construction (This account must be supported by a job cost subsidiary detailing the cost of each construction unit. (Refer to the Direct Construction Costs Subsidiary Ledger for subsidiary accounts detail.) It also includes finance and interest charges during construction. Don't include marketing costs or indirect construction costs in this account. When a house is closed, debit the cost to the
appropriate cost of sales account in the 3500 to 3700 series.)

1440 Indirect construction cost—A control account that requires a detailed breakdown in a subsidiary ledger showing the different types of cost accumulated in this account (Refer to the Indirect Construction Costs Subsidiary Ledger for subsidiary accounts detail.) Indirect construction costs are necessary costs of building that cannot be directly or easily attributed to a specific house or job. These costs are classified as part of the value of inventories because they contribute to the value of the work in progress. The IRS and GAAP generally require construction inventories to include a proportional share of indirect costs. When a sold house is closed, debit the proportional share of the cost in the 3500 to 3700 series. Alternatively, treat indirect costs by recording the cost within the 4000 series, an operating expense classification. To comply with IRS and GAAP requirements when using the alternative method, allocate the proportional share of indirect construction costs to the 1440 account.)

1500–1590 Finished Units and Other Inventory

1510 Finished units—Accumulated direct and indirect construction costs of units completed but not sold (Transfer from and credit accounts 1430, direct construction cost, and 1440, indirect construction cost, at the time of completion. The cost of the lot, accumulated in 1420, developed lots, is transferred to the 3500–3700 series at the time the sale is closed.)

1520 Model homes—Cost includes lot cost and direct and indirect construction costs of houses used as models (Upon completion of a model, transfer the costs to this account from 1420, developed lots; 1430, direct construction cost; and 1440, indirect construction cost, by debiting account 1520 and crediting accounts 1420, 1430, and 1440 by the respective amounts. Upon sale of model, transfer and debit costs to the 3500–3700 series and credit 1520.)

1530 Trade-ins and repossessions—The cost of any trade-ins acquired during a sales transaction and that are held for resale, but not held as investment, including refurbishing until sold (Transfer cost to 3660, cost of sales, trade-ins, when the units are closed.)

1600–1690 Other Current Assets

1610 Refundable deposits—Deposits paid to and held by municipalities, utilities, and other businesses for performance or completion of operation. (Include refundable plan deposits.)

1620 Prepaid expenses—Unexpired portions of expenses applicable to future periods, for items such as insurance, rent, commitment fees, interest and taxes (Detailed accounts for prepayments may be provided by using an additional sub-ledger or adding a two-digit subclass to the main account number.)

1630 Employee advances—Debit for a salary advance and credit when advance is deducted from payroll or repaid by employee

1650 Due from affiliates or subsidiaries—Short-term receivables due from affiliates or subsidiary companies

1660 Due from officers, stockholders, owners, or partners—Amounts currently due from officers, stockholders, owners, or partners of the business

1690 Other current assets—Miscellaneous current assets not otherwise classified

1700–1790 Investments and Other Assets

1710 Investments, long-term—Stocks, bonds, and other securities to be held as long term investments (By using an additional sub-ledger or two-digit subclass, each type of investment can be maintained in a separate account.)

1720 Cash surrender value of officers' life insurance—Accumulated net cash surrender value; net of any outstanding loans on life insurance carried on the officers of the business 1730 Investments in affiliated entities—Capital stock of affiliated companies, subsidiaries, partnerships and joint ventures (A company's portion of the equity or loss generated by the affiliated entity should be debited, income, or credited, loss, to this account on a periodic basis. The offsetting entry should be debited or credited to 9100, income from partnerships, joint ventures, S-corporations, and limited liability corporations, provided that the investing company can exercise significant influence—usually more than 20% of the voting power— over the operations of the affiliated entity.)

1750 Mortgage notes receivable, long-term—Amounts of mortgages that are due after the next fiscal year end

1760 Due from affiliated companies or subsidiaries, long-term—Amounts due from affiliated companies or subsidiaries that are to be carried for a long period

1780 Organization cost—Legal fees, corporate charter fees, and other organization costs that are normally capitalized (Credit amortization of these fees directly to this account.)

1800–1890 Property, Plant, and Equipment

1810 Land—Cost of land acquired for the purpose of constructing company offices and warehouses and held for investment (Land held for future development should be included in 1320, land held for development.)

1820 Buildings—Costs relating to offices, warehouses, field offices, field warehouse, and other company structures used in the operation of the business

1825 Rental property—Cost of property owned and managed by the company and held for investment (Buildings used in the operation of the business should be classified in 1820, buildings.)

1827 Recreation amenities—Property the company retains for ownership and operation (Include property to be turned over to a home owners' association in 1430, direct construction cost.

1830 Office furniture and equipment—Cost of office furniture, fixtures, and small equipment used by administrative and office personnel

1840 Vehicles—Cost of automobiles and trucks owned by the business

1850 Construction equipment—The cost of all construction equipment, excluding licensed motor vehicles (Charge or debit small tools of nominal value to 1440, indirect construction cost, or 4560, small tools and supplies.)

1870 Model home furnishings—Cost of model home furniture and furnishings

1880 Leasehold improvements—Cost of improvements made to leased property

1890 Computer equipment and software—Cost of computer hardware and software (They may be segregated to improve tracking.)

1900–1999 Accumulated Depreciation

1920 Accumulated depreciation, buildings—Accumulated depreciation on assets carried in 1820, Buildings

1925 Accumulated depreciation, rental properties—Accumulated depreciation on rental properties carried in 1825, rental property

1927 Accumulated depreciation, recreation amenities—Accumulated depreciation on property carried in 1827, recreation amenities

1930 Accumulated depreciation, office furniture and equipment—Accumulated depreciation on assets carried in 1830, office furniture and equipment

1940 Accumulated depreciation, vehicles—Accumulated depreciation on assets carried in 1840, vehicles

1950 Accumulated depreciation, construction equipment—Accumulated depreciation on assets carried in 1850, construction equipment

1970 Accumulated depreciation, model home furnishings—Accumulated depreciation on assets carried in 1870, model home furnishings

1980 Accumulated depreciation, leasehold improvements—Accumulated depreciation on assets carried in 1880, Leasehold improvements

1990 Accumulated depreciation, computer equipment and software—Accumulated depreciation on assets carried in 1890, computer equipment and software

<u>2000–2990 Liabilities and Owners' Equity</u>

2000–2090 Deposits by Customers

2010 Contract deposits—Down payments, earnest money, and deposits on contracts (Transfer and credit the deposit to the appropriate account in the 3000–3400 series, Sales and Revenues, when the sale is closed, and debit 2010, contract deposits.)

2030 Tenant security deposit—Refundable tenant deposits held to secure proper care of unit

2040 Advance rent collected—Rent collected from tenants that relate to a future period. (When the rental income is earned, debit this account, and credit 3200, rental property income.)

2100–2190 Accounts Payable

2110 Accounts payable, trade—Amounts payable on open account to suppliers and trade contractors

2120 Retentions payable—Amounts withheld from trade contractors until final completion and approval of their work

2190 Accounts payable, other—Other short-term open accounts due to non-trade individuals or companies

2200–2290 Notes Payable

2200 Line of credit payable—Outstanding balance on revolving line of credit

2220 Acquisitions and development loans payable—Control account for all loans from lending institutions for acquisition and development costs (Detail accounts for each acquisition or development may be provided by using an additional sub-ledger or a two- digit subclass to the main account number.)

2230 Construction loans payable—Control account for all loans from lending institutions for construction financing (Detail accounts for each construction loan payable may be provided by using an additional sub-ledger or a two-digit subclass to the main account number.)

2240 Current portion of long-term debt—Portion of principal payments included in 2510, long-term notes payable, and 2530, mortgage notes payable, that are due on notes to be paid within one year

2290 Notes payable, other—Notes payable to banks, other financial institutions, and other individuals that are due within one year

2300–2490 Other Current Liabilities

2310 Social Security and Medicare—Accumulated Social Security (FICA) and Medicare taxes withheld from employee payroll (This account is also used to accrue the employer portion of these taxes.)

2320 Federal payroll tax, withheld and accrued—Accumulated federal taxes withheld from employee payroll and owed to the federal government

2330 State and local payroll tax, withheld and accrued—Accumulated state taxes withheld from employee payroll and owed to state government (Credit funds withheld from employee pay, and debit payments to the state income tax division. Also include disability and other state withholding taxes. For multiple states, cities, or other local government withholdings, you may set up a separate account, or use a two-digit sub- account.)

2340 Other payroll withholdings—Other accumulated amounts withheld from employee payroll, such as employees' share of health insurance costs (Credit funds withheld from employee payroll, and debit payments to the proper agencies.)

2345 Union withholding and benefits payable—Accumulated amounts withheld from employee payroll in accordance with a collective bargaining agreement (This account can also be used to accrue employer liability for union benefits such as pension and welfare, training, health insurance, and other required benefits. To accrue benefits, credit this account and debit 4150, union benefits. Debit this account for payments to the union or appropriate fund.)

2350 Sales and use taxes payable—Credit amount of tax received from purchasers and debit payments to the taxing authority (Note that taxes paid on material used in construction are debited to 1430, direct construction cost, or 3830, building material.) 2360 Real estate taxes payable—Credit the company's liability for real estate taxes incurred to date, and debit payments to the taxing authority

2370 Income taxes payable—Credit for accrual of the company's current liability for federal and state income and franchise taxes and debit payments to the taxing authorities

2390 Accrued interest payable—Credit interest accrued and payable and debit payments

2400 Accrued salaries and wages payable—Control account for accrued salaries and wages (Credit accrued salaries and wages and debit payments made.)

2410 Accrued commissions payable—Commissions earned but not yet paid (Credit the amount of commission due and debit payments.)

2411 Accrued pension and profit-sharing expenses—Pension and profit sharing earned but not yet paid (Credit amount due and debit payments.)

2420 Workers' Compensation insurance payable—Amounts withheld from payment to trade contractors for Workers' Compensation insurance but not yet paid (This account can also accrue the employers' liability for Workers' Compensation for their employees.)

2425 Other accrued expenses—The liability for expenses that have been incurred, but invoices have not yet been received, or the expense has not been paid, such as professional fees, bonuses, commissions, and vacations (Detailed accounts for other accrued expenses may be provided by using an additional sub-ledger or adding a two-digit subclass to the main account number.)

2430 Deferred income—Advance payments made by tenants or other sources for which income is not yet earned (Credit advance payments to this account. Debit the account when the revenue is earned, and credit the appropriate income account.)

2440 Due to affiliated companies or subsidiaries—Amounts currently due to affiliated or subsidiary companies

2450 Due to officers, stockholders, owners, partners—Amounts currently due to officers, stockholders, owners, and partners

2480 Billings in excess of costs—Usually used by remodelers, custom builders, and commercial builders to record charges that exceed estimated costs (sometimes referred to as overbilling), using the percentage of completion method of accounting

2490 Other current liabilities—Miscellaneous current liabilities not otherwise classified

2500–2890 Long-Term Liabilities

2510 Long-term notes payable—Control account for notes on vehicles, equipment, and other assets used in operations (Include current portion in 2240, current portion of long- term debt. Detailed accounts for long-term payable liabilities may be provided by using an additional sub-ledger or a two-digit subclass to the main account number.)

2530 Mortgage notes payable—Control account for mortgages on rental property and land and buildings used in operations (Include current portion in 2240, current portion of long-term debt. Detailed accounts for mortgage notes payable may be provided by using an additional sub-ledger or a two-digit subclass to the main account number.)

2600 Deferred income taxes payable—Income taxes due on deferred income

2610 Due to affiliated companies or subsidiaries, long-term—Amounts due to affiliated companies or subsidiaries that are to be carried for a long-term period.

2620 Due to officers, stockholders, owners, partners, long-term—Amounts due to company officers, stockholders, owners and partners to be carried for a long-term period

2700 Other long-term liabilities—Long-term liabilities not otherwise classified

2900–2990 Owners' Equity

2900 Common stock—Par value or stated value of stock outstanding

2910 Additional paid in capital—Amounts received in excess of par or stated value of stock
2920 Retained earnings—Prior years' accumulation of profits or losses
2930 Treasury stock—The corporation's own capital stock which has been issued and then reacquired by the corporation by either purchase or gift
2940 Unrealized holding loss—Represents cumulative unrealized loss on investments or marketable securities (Investments or marketable securities should be adjusted to the market value on an annual or periodic basis.)
2950 Partnership or proprietorship account—A separate account for each partner, indicating accumulated equity to date (Detailed accounts for partnership or proprietorship account may be provided by using an additional sub-ledger or adding a two-digit subclass to the main account number.)
2960 Distributions, dividends, and draws—Accumulated owners' withdrawals for period (Maintain a separate account for each owner. Debit distributions, dividends, and draws to this account. At the end of the fiscal year, close the account by crediting this account and debiting the amounts to 2920, retained earnings, or 2950, partnership or proprietorship account, as applicable. Detailed accounts for distributions, dividends, and draws may be provided by using an additional sub-ledger or adding a two-digit subclass to the main account number.)

3000–3990 Sales, Revenues, and Cost of Sales

3000–3490 Sales and Revenues

3000 Sales, land held for development—Revenues earned from sales of raw land not yet subdivided, and without improvements
3050 Sales, developed lots—Revenues earned from sales of partially or fully developed lots
3100 Sales, single-family, speculative—Revenues earned from sales of spec houses
3110 Sales, single-family, production—Revenues earned from sales of production houses 3120 Sales, single-family, custom designed—Revenues earned from sales of custom houses
3125 Sales, single-family, custom, no land—Revenues earned from sales of houses built under contract on land owned by someone other than the builder
3130 Sales, residential remodeling—Revenues earned from sales of residential remodeling work
3133 Sales, commercial and industrial remodeling—Revenues earned from sales of commercial and industrial remodeling work
3135 Sales, insurance restoration—Revenues earned from sales of insurance restoration work
3137 Sales, repairs—Revenues earned from sales of repair work
3140 Sales, multifamily—Revenues earned from sales of multifamily units
3150 Sales, commercial and Industrial—Revenues earned from sales of new commercial and industrial construction
3160 Sales, trade-Ins, and repossessions—Revenues earned from sales of houses originally received as partial payment on another sale or repossessions
3190 Sales, other—Revenues earned from sales of construction activities not otherwise classified
3195 Cancellation fees—Forfeiture of contract deposits
3200 Rental property income—Revenues earned from rental of investment property and office space

3210 Common area reimbursements—Revenues earned from tenant reimbursement of common area expenses (Common area expenses should be charged to the applicable account within the 7000 series. Other reimbursements should be credited to 3220, other reimbursements.)

3220 Other reimbursements—Revenues earned from tenant reimbursement of expenses (Expenses incurred by the company should be charged to the applicable account within the 7000 series.)

3230 Parking fee income—Revenue earned from the rental of company-owned parking facilities

3240 Amenities facilities income—Revenue earned from rental and use charges for company-owned recreational facilities

3360 Construction management fee income—Revenues earned from construction management activities

3379 Design fees collected—Revenues earned from design activities

3400 Miscellaneous income—Revenues earned from sources not otherwise classified

3410 Interest income—Interest earned from certificates of deposits, savings accounts, and other sources

3420 Dividend income—Dividends earned from investments in stocks, bonds, and other sources

3450 Earned discounts—Cash discounts earned from payment on account within the time established by the supplier or trade contractor

3460 Earned rebates—Incentives received from manufacturer for use of their products 3490 Sales concessions and discounts—Accumulates the difference between the published sales price and the contract price (This account captures the impact of concessions on company margins. If this account is used, the published price is placed in the appropriate sales account, and concessions and discounts are debited here. This contra account is a reduction to sales.)

3500–3700 Cost of Sales

3500 Cost of sales, land held for development—Includes transfers from 1320, land held for development, at the time of sale (Credit 1320 and debit 3500, cost of sales, land held for development.)

3550 Cost of sales, developed lots—Allocated amount to be written off on lots sold (Credit 1420, if the lot was developed prior to purchase, or 1412, accumulated allocations, land and land development costs, if the company developed the lot. Debit 3550, cost of sales, developed lots.)

3600 Cost of sales, single-family, speculative—Direct construction costs related to sales of homes recorded in 3100, sales, single-family, speculative (Transfer from and credit 1430, direct construction cost. Debit 3600.)

3610 Cost of sales, single-family, production—Direct construction costs of houses built under contract (Transfer from Account 1430, Direct construction cost. Debit 3610, cost of sales, single-family, production.)

3620 Cost of sales, single-family, custom designed—Direct construction costs of custom houses (Transfer from 1430, direct construction cost, if applicable. Debit 3620, cost of sales, single-family, custom designed.)

3625 Cost of sales, single family, custom, no land—Direct construction costs of custom homes built on land owned by someone other than the builder (Transfer from 1430, direct construction cost, if applicable. Debit 3625, cost of sales, single-family, custom, no land.) 3630 Cost of sales, remodeling—Direct construction costs of remodeling (Transfer from 1430, direct construction cost, if applicable. Debit 3630, cost of sales, remodeling. Alternatively, use the 3800 series to directly post remodeling costs to cost of sales.)

3633 Cost of sales, commercial and industrial remodeling—Direct construction costs of commercial and industrial jobs (Transfer from 1430, direct construction cost, if applicable. Debit 3633, cost of sales, commercial and industrial remodeling.)

3635 Cost of sales, insurance restoration—Direct costs for insurance restoration work (Transfer from 1430, direct construction cost, if applicable. Debit 3635, cost of sales, insurance restoration.)

3637 Cost of sales, repairs—Direct costs for repairs (Transfer from 1430, direct construction cost, if applicable. Debit 3637, cost of sales, repairs.)

3640 Cost of sales, multifamily—Direct construction costs of multifamily units sold (Transfer from 1430 direct construction cost. Debit 3640 cost of sales, multifamily.)

3650 Cost of sales, commercial and industrial—Direct construction costs of commercial and industrial jobs (Transfer from 1430, direct construction cost, if applicable. Debit 3650, cost of sales, commercial and industrial.)

3660 Cost of sales, trade-ins—Trade-in allowance and refurbishing (Transfer from 1530, trade-ins and repossessions, at the time of sale. Debit 3660, cost of sales, trade-ins.)

3690 Cost of sales, other—Costs incurred to generate income from sources not otherwise classified

3700 Direct construction cost for prior periods—Cost adjustments to cost of sales for charges or credits from prior period closings (These adjustments are for changes in cost that have not been accounted for after closing an individual unit.)

3800–3899 Costs of Construction

The following accounts can be used by remodelers and builders to directly post construction costs to cost of sales, instead of posting direct construction costs to 1430, direct construction cost.)

3810 Direct labor—Includes the gross wages paid to lead carpenters and crews engaged in the remodeling process

3820 Labor burden—Payroll taxes and Workers' Compensation insurance, as well as other items such as health insurance, life and disability insurance that relate to gross wages paid to the field crew (Also, includes vacation, holiday, sick days, and other paid days off for the field crew.)

3830 Building material—Cost of materials used on a remodeling project (Also includes all freight and taxes paid on the material in this account.)

3840 Trade contractors—Cost of trade contractors used on a specific remodeling project 3850 Rental equipment—Cost of rental equipment used on a specific remodeling project 3860 Other direct construction costs—Includes cost of small tools consumed on a specific remodeling project, cost of permits and fees for a particular project, and any other direct construction costs not otherwise classified

3870 Professional design fees—Costs paid to architects, engineers, interior designers, certified kitchen designers, and bath designers for use on a specific remodeling job (Also includes in-house design salaries, wages, and the related labor burden in this account if they are incurred on a specific remodeling job.)

4000–4990 Indirect Construction Cost

The 4000 series of accounts is an alternative to 1440, indirect construction cost. The 4000 series allows a detailed breakdown of accounts in the general ledger while maintaining a four-digit numerical code. The indirect costs accumulated in these accounts must still be allocated to houses or specific jobs held in inventory to comply with GAAP and IRS regulations.

4000–4090 Salaries and Wages

Salaries and wages of personnel directly engaged in the construction process, but not identified with a specific unit

4010 Superintendents—Salaries of supervisory personnel for time spent in organizing, planning, or supervising production crews (This category does not include wages of personnel who work on specific jobs and their crews.)

4020 Laborers—Wages paid to laborers on construction that cannot be charged to a specific job. (If possible, labor should be estimated, budgeted, and charged to a specific job.)

4030 Production manager—Salaries paid to the supervisors of superintendents

4040 Architects, drafters, estimators, purchasers—Salaries and wages of persons who perform these duties for construction jobs (If this function is a department unto itself, each person's job may be broken down into a separate account.)

4050 Warranty and customer service manager—Salaries of employees responsible for the warranty and service function

4060 Warranty and customer service wages—Labor incurred to repair, replace, or service any item on a particular unit after possession by owner

4070 Other indirect construction wages—Salaries and wages of personnel such as timekeepers, security guards, and quality control inspectors who are involved in the construction process but not identified with specific units

4990 Absorbed indirect costs—Used as a contra account to allocate the proportional share of indirect construction cost to work in process inventories to comply with IRS and GAAP requirements (This contra account requires a year-end closing adjustment, which is usually handled by an accountant.)

4100–4190 Payroll Taxes and Benefits

4110 Payroll taxes—The accumulated share of FICA, unemployment, Medicare, Social Security, and other company-paid taxes related to salaries and wages charged as indirect cost

4120 Workers' Compensation insurance—Insurance premiums for individual construction workers

4130 Health and accident insurance—Premiums for health and accident insurance for indirect construction workers

4140 Retirement, pension, profit sharing—Employer contributions to retirement, pension, and profit-sharing plans for indirect construction workers

4150 Union benefits—Benefits related to indirect construction workers in accordance with a collective bargaining agreement

4190 Other benefits—Benefits related to salaries and wages charged as indirect costs not otherwise classified

4200–4290 Field Office Expenses

Maintenance and repairs, utilities, telephone and other expenses incidental to a field office, including erection and moving. The field office is often a trailer; if the office is in model, include these expenses in the 6600 series of accounts (model home maintenance). 4210 Rent, field office—Rent for field office

4230 Repairs and maintenance, field office—Repairs and maintenance of field office, including service contracts

4250 Utilities, field office—Heat, electricity and other utilities for field office

4260 Telephone, field office—Installation and monthly charges for field office telephone and related communications equipment

4265 Mobile phones, pagers, and radios, field office—Purchase and monthly charges for cellular phones, pagers, and field radios for construction personnel

4290 Other field office expenses—Expenses for field office not included in other categories

4300–4390 Field Warehouse and Storage Expense

Costs incurred in material handling and storage if materials are not delivered to the jobsite by supplier

4310 Rent, field warehouse and storage—Rent on warehouse and storage facilities

4330 Repairs and maintenance, field warehouse and storage—Repairs and maintenance of warehouse and storage facilities, including service contracts

4350 Utilities, field warehouse and storage—Heat, electricity and other utilities for warehouse and storage facilities

4360 Telephone, field warehouse and storage—Installation and monthly charges for telephone in warehouse and storage

4400–4490 Construction Vehicles, Travel, and Entertainment

4410 Lease payments, construction vehicles—Payments on leased or rented vehicles used by construction personnel

4420 Mileage reimbursement—Payment to field personnel for use of their private vehicles

4430 Repairs and maintenance, construction vehicles—Repair and maintenance costs for automobiles and trucks used by construction personnel (Includes both minor and major work.)

4440 Operating expenses, construction vehicles—Fuel, oil, and lubrication expenses for automobiles and trucks used by construction personnel

4450 Taxes, licenses, insurance, construction vehicles—Property damage and liability insurance, licenses, fees, and taxes on vehicles used by construction personnel

4460 Travel, construction department—Travel expenses incurred by construction personnel

4470 Customer business entertainment, construction—Business-related entertainment expenses incurred by construction personnel

4480 Training and education, construction—Training and education expenses incurred by construction personnel

4490 Recruiting fees and expenses, construction—Expenses associated with the hiring of construction personnel

4500–4590 Construction Equipment

Costs of maintaining and operating construction equipment

4510 Rent, construction equipment—Payments on leased or rented equipment

4530 Repairs and maintenance, construction equipment—Repair and maintenance costs on equipment

4540 Operating expenses, construction equipment—Fuel, oil, and lubrication expenses on equipment

4550 Taxes and insurance, construction equipment—Taxes and insurance required on equipment

4560 Small tools and supplies—Cost of items such as hand tools, shovels, skill saws, small power tools, and extension cords, used in construction

4600–4690 Expenses for Maintaining Unsold Units and Units under Construction

Costs applicable to units under construction, prior to delivery to customer

4610 Temporary utilities—Utility hook-up costs and utility bills related to units under construction (Custom and small-volume builders may consider classifying these costs as part of direct construction cost.)

4620 Trash maintenance—Cost of trash hauling, dumpsters, and other equipment necessary for construction site maintenance

4640 Lawn care—Costs required to maintain the lawn prior to transfer to customer

4650 Utilities, completed units—Utility cost and hookups for finished units held in inventory and awaiting sale

4660 Repairs and maintenance, completed units—Cost of repair and maintenance to any unit held in inventory for sale

4700–4790 Warranty and Customer Service

4710 Salaries and wages, warranty—Labor incurred to repair, replace, or service any item after possession of a unit by owner

4720 Material, warranty—Price of materials to repair, replace, or service any item after possession of a unit by owner

4730 Trade contractor, warranty—Cost of trade contractor, incurred to repair, replace, or service any item after possession of a unit by owner

4790 Other warranty expenses—Costs—other than labor, materials, or trade con- tractors—incurred to repair, replace, or service any item after possession of a unit by owner

4800–4890 Depreciation Expenses

4820 Depreciation, construction office—Depreciation expense of construction of fire equipment

4830 Depreciation, warehouse—Depreciation expense of warehouse

4840 Depreciation, construction vehicles—Depreciation expense of construction vehicles 4850 Depreciation, construction equipment—Depreciation expense of construction equipment

4900–4990 Other

4910 Insurance and bonding expenses—Cost of obtaining insurance or bonding for construction projects and properties

4920 Builder's risk insurance—Cost of obtaining builder's risk insurance (Custom and small-volume builders may be more inclined to treat this as a direct cost.)

4990 Absorbed indirect costs—To comply with IRS and GAAP requirements and allocate the proportional share of indirect construction cost to work in process inventories (This contra account requires a year-end closing adjustment, which is usually handled by an accountant.)

5000–5990 Financing Expenses

5000–5090 Interest

5010 Interest on line of credit—Interest expense on loans held by banks and other lenders for operating capital

5020 Interest on notes payable—Interest expense on notes payable for fixed assets such as office buildings and vehicles

5030 Interest expense on developed lots—Interest expense on developed lots not currently under construction

5040 Interest incurred on construction loans—Interest expense paid during the building of a house (To comply with IRS and GAAP requirements, interest on construction loans must be capitalized during the construction period. If interest is posted to this account, allocate the proportionate share of interest to work-in-process inventories to comply with IRS and GAAP requirements at year end.)

5050 Interest on completed speculative inventory—Interest expense paid on completed speculative homes before closing on the units

5090 Interest expense, other—Other interest paid or accrued

5100–5190 Construction Loan Points and Fees

5120 Points and fees—Expenses paid on points and fees for construction loans

5130 Appraisal and related fees—Service charges paid for appraisal of property related to construction loans

5140 Inspection fees—Fees for inspection by lenders

5200–5290 Closing Costs

Closing costs related to the sale of finished houses

5210 Closing costs—Closing costs related to the sale of finished houses (including property and real estate taxes) paid by the seller (Custom and small volume builders may charge closing costs as a direct expense. If they are paid on buyer's behalf as a concession, include in 6930, sales concessions.)

5220 Title and recording—Fees charged for searching and recording and for title insurance

5230 Loan fees—Origination or standby fees on permanent financing commitments

6000–6990 Sales and Marketing Expenses

This section of the operating expense chart of accounts is reserved for sales and marketing expenses that may be written off as period expenses.

6000–6090 Sales Salaries, Commissions

6010 Compensation, sales manager—Compensation, including bonuses or incentives, for sales managers

6030 Salaries, sales personnel—Salaries for noncommissioned activities, excluding draws against present or future commissions

6040 Sales commissions, in-house—Commissions paid to employees (Remodelers sometimes charge these commissions as a direct cost.)

6050 Sales commissions, outside—Commissions paid to sales agents and others not employed by the company

6090 Other sales office salaries and wages—Salaries and wages for clerical and other personnel who work directly for the sales department or sales office, including hostesses and sales assistants

6100–6190 Payroll Taxes and Benefits, Sales and Marketing

Payroll taxes and benefits associated with salaries and wages of the sales and marketing department or sales office employees

6110 Payroll taxes, sales and marketing—Accumulated share of FICA, unemployment, and other taxes relating to salaries and wages of sales and marketing personnel

6120 Workers' compensation insurance, sales and marketing—Insurance premiums on salaries and wages of sales and marketing personnel

6130 Health and accident insurance, sales and marketing—Premiums for health and accident insurance for sales and marketing personnel

6140 Retirement, pension, profit-sharing plans, sales and marketing—Employer contributions paid to retirement, pension, and profit-sharing plans for sales and marketing personnel

6190 Other benefits, sales and marketing—Benefits relating to salaries and wages of sales and marketing personnel

6200–6290 Sales Office Expenses

Operating costs related to a separate sales office or design center. (If the sales office is in a model home, include expenses in the 6660–6690 series, model home maintenance.) 6210 Rent, sales office—Rental of sales office

6230 Repairs and maintenance, sales office—Cost of all interior and exterior sales office building repairs and maintenance, including interior remodeling not capitalized, janitorial service, landscaping, and window washing

6250 Utilities, sales office—Heat and other utilities for sales office

6260 Telephone, sales office—Installation and monthly charges, both land-line and cell phones for sales office

6270 Supplies, sales office—Office supplies used by sales office staff

6300–6395 Advertising and Sales Promotion

6310 Print advertising—Classified and display advertising expenses

6320 Radio advertising—Expenses for radio time and related services

6325 Television advertising—Expenses for television time and related services

6330 Internet fees, Web page design and maintenance expense—Expenses for Internet fees, design of Web pages and related maintenance

6340 Brochures and catalogs—Cost of designing and printing brochures and catalogs 6350 Signs—Expenses for photography, typography, printing, artwork, copywriting, materials, and supplies required to make signs

6355 Billboards—Fees paid for art and advertising on billboards

6365 Promotions—Fees paid for special programs and items, such as move-in gifts

6370 Agency commissions—Fees paid to agencies that assist in setting up advertising programs

6380 Multiple listing fees—Payments to a centralized brokerage service

6390 Public relations—Fees paid to public relations firms for press releases and other publicity

6395 Referral fees—Payments for referrals

6400–6490 Sales Vehicles, Travel, and Entertainment

6410 Lease payments, sales vehicles—Payments on leased or rented vehicles used for sales and marketing personnel

6420 Mileage reimbursement—Payment to sales and marketing personnel for use of their private vehicles

6430 Repairs and maintenance, sales vehicles—Repair and maintenance costs for the company's automobiles used by sales and marketing personnel, including both minor and major work

6440 Operating expense, sales vehicles—Fuel, oil, and lubrication costs

6450 Taxes, licenses, insurance, sales vehicles—Property damage and liability insurance, licenses, fees, and taxes on company vehicles used by sales and marketing personnel 6460 Travel, sales and marketing—Travel expenses incurred by sales and marketing personnel

6470 Customer business entertainment—Entertainment expenses incurred by sales and marketing personnel

6600–6690 Model Home Maintenance

6610 Rent or lease payments, model home furnishings—Costs of renting or leasing model home furnishings

6620 Model home rent or lease payments—Costs of renting or leasing the model home

6625 Decorating fees, model home—Fees for decorating services

6630 Repairs and maintenance, model homes—Repairs, maintenance, and decoration expenses resulting from use, damage, or minor changes to the model or its furnishings 6650 Utilities, model homes—Heat, electricity, water and sewer expenses

6670 Lawn and landscaping care, model homes—Labor and material costs for lawn maintenance, including mowing, watering, seeding or sodding, and fertilizing lawns and pruning other vegetation

6680 Cleanup, model homes—Costs relating to window washing and daily cleanup 6690 Interest on model homes—Interest paid after completion of the model home(s) *6700–6790 Sales and Marketing Fees*

6710 Market research and consultation—Fees for market research and consultation 6720 Interior design fee—Fees paid for outside designers to assist buyers with their selections 6770 Recruiting fees and expenses, sales and marketing personnel—Expenses associated with the hiring of sales and marketing personnel

6780 Training and education expenses—Cost of travel and registration fees for seminars and conventions, meals and lodging expenses, in-house programs, literature, and materials (Also includes expenses incurred for conventions and trade shows, as well as national, state, and local association meetings.)

6800–6890 Depreciation

6810 Depreciation, sales office—Depreciation on sales office

6830 Depreciation, sales vehicles—Depreciation on sales and marketing vehicles

6870 Depreciation, model home furnishings and decorations—Depreciation on model home furnishings and decorations

6900–6990 Other Marketing Expenses

6930 Sales concessions—Announced discounts and other incentives (such as gifts and travel incentives) provided to customers as part of marketing and sales strategy

6940 Buy downs—Refunds of interest and points issued to customers during the sales process

6999 Other sales and marketing expenses—Sales and marketing expenses not otherwise classified

<u>7000–7990 Operating and Management Expense, Rental Operations</u>

7000–7090 Property Management

7010 Compensation, property manager—Compensation, including bonuses and incentives, for managers of property management personnel

7030 Salaries and wages, property management personnel—Direct salaries and wages for non-commission activities, excluding draws against present and future commissions, which should be debited to 7040, commissions, in-house, or 7050, commissions, outside.) 7040 Commissions, in-house—Commissions paid to property management personnel employed by the company for leasing of rental property

7050 Commissions, outside—Commissions paid to sales agents and others not employed by the company for leasing of rental property

7060 Salaries and wages, maintenance personnel—Wages and salaries of company personnel assigned to the maintenance and repair of rental property (To track the different types of work performed by maintenance personnel—such as janitorial service, landscaping, and repair—a builder may want to add a 1 or 2 digit suffix to this account number for each type of work performed. For example, this account could include 706001 and so on.)

7070 Payroll taxes and benefits, rental operations—Cost of the company's FICA, Medicare, and federal and state unemployment insurance for rental personnel

7072 Workers' compensation insurance, rental—Insurance premiums on salaries and wages of rental personnel

7073 Health and accident insurance, rental—Premiums for health and accident insurance for rental personnel

7074 Retirement, pension, and profit-sharing plans, rental—Employer contributions to retirement, pension, and profit-sharing plans for rental personnel

7079 Other benefits, rental—Salaries and wages for in-house clerical and other personnel involved in property management activities not otherwise classified

7100–7190 Rental Expenses

7110 Advertising—Advertising costs directly related to the renting of individual rental units

7130 Credit reports—Charges from credit bureaus for reports about prospective tenants 7190 Other rental expenses—Rental expenses not otherwise classified, such as concessions to tenants

7200–7290 Administrative Expense, Rental Operations

7220 Management and service fees—Fees paid to outside firms for the management and operation of a company-owned property management activity

7230 Office expenses—Costs of maintaining an office for a property management activity, including rent, supplies, and postage

7240 Telephone—Standard monthly charges and long distance costs directly related to a property management activity

7250 Tenant bad debts—Write-off of past-due rents receivable from tenants

7260 Collection costs—Costs incurred in pursuing collection of past-due rents receivable, including collection agency fees

7290 Other administrative expenses—Administrative expenses of a property management activity not otherwise classified

7300–7390 Professional Services, Rental Operations

7310 Legal services—Charges for legal counsel for all services relating to a property management activity

7320 Accounting services—Charges for preparation of financial statements, tax advice, and other services rendered by an outside accounting firm relating to a property management activity

7330 Market research—Charges from consulting firms or individuals for market research relating to a property management activity

7390 Other professional services, rental operations—Professional service costs for a property management activity not otherwise classified

7400–7490 Operating Expense, Rental Operations

7410 Utilities—Gas, electricity, water and sewer service, and other utilities for rental buildings

7420 Engineering—Payroll and other costs associated with engineering activities related to property management

7430 Janitorial—Costs for janitorial services for property management activity

7440 Trash removal service—Costs of contracted services for the removal of trash and other waste from related buildings

7450 Exterminating—Supplies and other costs associated with extermination services supplied by company personnel or an independent contractor

7460 Snow removal—Supplies and other costs associated with snow removal services supplied by company personnel or an independent contractor

7470 Other contractual services—Costs of services such as sign painting and design provided under contract for a property management activity and not otherwise classified 7480 Vehicles and equipment, rental operations—Cost of leasing and operating equipment for use at the rental property

7490 Other rental operations expenses—Operating costs of a rental property not otherwise classified

7500–7590 Taxes and Insurance, Rental Operations

7510 Real estate property taxes—Local taxes on rental property, land, improvements, and buildings

7520 Personal property taxes—Local taxes assessed on business-owned personal property at a rental property

7530 Franchise taxes—State tax on rental property for privilege of doing business

7540 License fees—Local fees for licenses, registrations, and permits

7560 Workers' compensation insurance—Costs for Workers' compensation insurance 7570 Insurance, rental operations—Costs for general liability, property damage, and extended fire insurance

7590 Other taxes and insurance, rental operations—Tax and insurance costs not otherwise classified

7600–7690 Maintenance and Repair Expense, Rental Operations

7610 Tenant redecorating, rental operations—Payroll, supplies, and all other costs associated with redecorating rental units; including services supplied by company personnel or independent contractors

7630 Maintenance contracts and services, rental operations—Charges from independent contractors for maintenance and repair services

7640 Ground maintenance and repairs, rental operations—Costs of maintaining rental property grounds, including landscaping provided by company personnel or independent contractors

7650 Vehicle maintenance and repairs, rental operations—Labor and material costs associated with the general maintenance and repair of company-owned vehicles used at a rental property

7660 Equipment maintenance and repairs, rental operations—Labor and materials costs incurred by company personnel or outside contractors for the maintenance and repair of equipment used at a rental property

7670 Amenities maintenance and repairs, rental operations—Labor and material costs incurred by company personnel or outside contractors for the maintenance and repair of recreational facilities at a rental property

7700–7790 Financing Expenses, Rental Operations

7710 Interest on mortgage payable—Interest charges associated with a permanent mortgage loan on rental buildings

7720 Interest on long-term notes payable—Interest charges from notes payable associated with rental operations

7800–7890 Depreciation Expense, Rental Operations

7810 Depreciation, building—Depreciation for buildings such as rental properties

7820 Depreciation, maintenance equipment—Depreciation for company-owned equipment used for maintaining rental premises

7830 Depreciation, vehicles—Depreciation for company-owned vehicles and maintenance equipment used at rental properties

7840 Depreciation, furniture and fixtures—Depreciation for company-owned furniture, fixtures, office machines, and office equipment used for rental operations

7850 Depreciation, amenities—Depreciation for rental property recreational facilities 7890 Other depreciation—Depreciation for assets used in rental operations not otherwise classified

7900–7990 Other Management and Operating Expenses – Management and operating expenses not otherwise classified

8000–8990 General and Administrative Expenses

8000–8090 Salaries and Wages

8010 Salaries, owners—Total compensation paid to owners, including salaries and bonuses

8020 Salaries, officers—Total compensation paid to nonowner company officers, including salaries and bonuses

8030 Salaries, management—Total compensation paid to upper- and middle- management personnel, other than owners or officers, including salaries and bonuses 8050 Salaries and wages, office and clerical—Total compensation paid to clerical and other personnel below the managerial level, including salaries, wages, and bonuses

8090 Other general and administrative salaries and wages—Total compensation paid to general and administrative personnel, and those not otherwise classified, including salaries, wages, and bonuses

8100–8190 Payroll Taxes and Benefits

8110 Payroll taxes—Cost of the company's FICA, Medicare, federal and state unemployment insurance, and other local taxes that relate to administrative salaries and wages

8120 Workers' compensation insurance—Insurance premiums for Workers' compensation, paid by the employer, for administrative and hourly employees

8130 Health and accident insurance—Health and accident insurance premiums, paid by the employer for administrative personnel

8140 Retirement, pension, profit-sharing plans—Employee contributions to retirement, pension, and profit-sharing plans for administrative personnel

8190 Other employee benefits—Benefits relating to salaries and wages of administrative personnel

8200–8290 Office Expenses

8210 Rent—Rental payments for administrative office space

8220 Office equipment rental—Rental payments on office equipment, cellular phones, and pagers for office personnel

8230 Repairs and maintenance, administrative office space—Costs of all interior and exterior administrative office building repairs and maintenance, including interior remodeling not capitalized, landscaping, janitorial service, and window washing

8240 Repairs and maintenance, administrative office equipment—All contracts and other charges for maintenance of office equipment

8250 Utilities, administrative office—Costs of utilities for the administrative offices

8260 Telephone, administrative office—Standard monthly fees and long distance charges, including cell phones, not applied to other functions or departments

8270 Office supplies, administrative office—Printing, stationery, and other office supplies 8280 Postage and deliveries—Postage, express mail, couriers, FedEx, UPS, and other delivery services

8290 Miscellaneous expenses, administrative office—Office expenses not otherwise classified, including monthly answering service fees and paging services

8300–8390 Technology and Computer Expenses

8310 Computer supplies—Paper and all supplies necessary for the operation of the computer system

8320 Leases, computer hardware—Payments on leased hardware

8330 Leases, computer software—Payments on leased software

8335 Software licensing and subscription fees—Expenses associated with software licensing and subscription fees

8340 Network and Web development expenses—Costs related to intranet and extranet 8350 Repairs and maintenance, computer equipment—Service contract or other payments for the maintenance of computer hardware

8360 Maintenance, computer software—Contract or other payments for the maintenance agreement of the systems software

8400–8490 Vehicle, Travel, and Entertainment

8410 Lease, administrative vehicles—Payments on leased or rental vehicles used by administrative personnel

8420 Mileage reimbursement—Payments to administrative personnel for use of their private vehicles

8430 Repairs and maintenance, administrative vehicles—Repair and maintenance costs of automobiles used by administrative personnel, including both minor and major work 8440 Operating expense, administrative vehicles—Vehicle fuel, oil, and lubrication costs 8450 Taxes, licenses, insurance, administrative vehicles—Taxes, licenses, fees, and property damage and liability insurance on vehicles used by administrative personnel 8460 Travel—Travel expenses incurred by administrative personnel

8470 Customer business expense—Entertainment expenses incurred by administrative personnel

8480 Meeting expenses—Expenses incurred by officers and employees representing the company at various groups, industry meetings, and other external events

8490 In-House meeting expenses—Expenses incurred in holding in-house meetings

8500–8590 Taxes

8510 Sales and use taxes—Taxes imposed by the state, county, and city on non-direct construction cost materials used within the city limits but purchased outside those borders 8520 Real estate taxes—Tax on property used for the company's offices and realty taxes not charged elsewhere

8530 Personal property taxes—Assessment of personal property owned by the company

8540 License fees—License, registration, municipal fees, and operating permits

8590 Other taxes—Taxes not otherwise classified, such as state tax on capitalization and franchise tax

8600–8690 Insurance

8610 Hazard insurance, property insurance—Fire insurance and extended coverage on buildings and contents

8630 General liability insurance—Costs of liability insurance, including general and product liability insurance excluding vehicles

8690 Other insurance—Insurance premiums not otherwise classified

8700–8790 Professional Services

8710 Accounting services—Audit charges and charges for assistance in the preparation of financial statements, tax advice, and other services rendered by an outside accounting firm 8720 Legal services—Charges submitted by legal counsel for services rendered

8730 Consulting services—Service bureau, time-sharing, or professional fees for services rendered

8770 Recruiting and hiring—Expenses associated with hiring administrative personnel

8790 Other professional expenses—Professional fees not otherwise classified

8800–8890 Depreciation Expenses

8810 Depreciation, buildings—Depreciation on company buildings such as administrative offices

8830 Depreciation, vehicles—Depreciation on company-owned vehicles used by administrative personnel

8840 Depreciation, furniture, and equipment—Depreciation on furniture, fixtures, office machines, and other equipment

8860 Amortization of leasehold improvements—Amortization of improvements to office buildings leased from another entity

8870 Depreciation, computer equipment and software—Deprecation for computer hardware and software programs (These items may be segregated for easier tracking and control.)

8880 Amortization of organization cost—Write-off of organization cost, including legal fees and corporate charter fees

8890 Depreciation, other—Depreciation and amortization charges not otherwise classified

8900–8990 General and Administrative Expense, Other

8900 Bad debts—Charges for uncollectible receivables (Credit 1280, allowance for doubtful accounts.)

8905 Legal settlement expenses—Expenses dictated by the court as a result of legal action

8910 Contributions—All charitable donations

8911 Contributions, political—All contributions made to political organizations and candidates (These contributions are generally not deductible.)

8920 Dues and subscriptions—Trade association dues and subscriptions for magazines, newspapers, trade journals, business publications, reports, and manuals

8950 Bank charges—Bank fees for miscellaneous charges. (Check printing should be charged to 8270, office supplies, administrative office.)

8960 Penalties and other nondeductible expenses—Tax penalties, fines, parking tickets 8990 Training and education expenses—Cost of travel and registration fees for seminars and conventions, meals and lodging expenses, in-house programs, literature, and materials (Also includes expenses incurred for conventions and trade shows, as well as national, state, and local association meetings.)

9000–9990 Other Income and Expenses

9100–9190 Other Income

Income derived from sources other than the primary activity of the business

9100 Income from partnerships, joint ventures, S corporations (S corps), and limited liability corporations (LLCs)—Income (loss) from participation in partnerships, joint ventures, S corps, and LLCs

9120 Loss from impairment write-downs of developed lots—Unrealized loss, created by the write-down of developed lots to reflect the lower of cost or market

9150 Gain or loss on sale of assets—Gain or loss (debit) on the sale of assets that had been used in the operation of the business, such as vehicles, computers, and office equipment 9190 Other—Income derived from sources other than the main activity of the business, including speaking and consulting fees, expert witness fees, home inspections, real estate commissions, and budgeting fees

9200–9290 Other expenses

Extraordinary expenses or expenses attributable to activities not related to the main activity of the business

9200 Extraordinary expenses—Expenses attributable to activities not related to the main activity of the business (Separate account numbers within this series can be set up to track different categories of other expenses.)

9300–9390 Provision for Income Taxes

Provision for federal and state taxes on current income

9300 Provision for federal income taxes 9320 Provision for state income taxes 9330 Provision for local income taxes

APPENDIX C

PRO FORMA FINANCIAL STATEMENTS

Appendix C contains copies of the following templates:

Instructions

Historical P&L – Builder

Historical P&L – Remodeler

Projected Balance Sheet

Projected Income Statement

Projected Work-In-Progress Detail

Projected Income Detail

Indirect Construction Cost Detail

Operating Budget

Projected Cash Flow

These copies are shown for illustration purposes. The Microsoft® Excel® workbook containing the actual spreadsheets for your use can be downloaded on the author's webpage.

Instructions

Historical P & L

Fill in these worksheet with numbers from your previous year's profit and loss statements

Projected Balance Sheet

Fill in this worksheet by following the Comments in the Comments Boxes.

Projected Income Statement

The Income Statement is filled in automatically when you complete filling in the information in the Projected Income Detail, Indirect Construction Costs, and Operating Budget worksheets.

Projected Work-In-Progress Detail

The Projected Work-In-Progress Detail worksheet is where you fill in the anticipated Cost of Construction and the amount of Customer Deposits, Customer Payments on Contract, Development and Acquistion Loans, and Construction Loan draws on "Revenue at Job Sale" jobs on which company owns the full assets of the job until closing such as.speculative homes, pre-sold homes on which the builder is carrying the construction loan, and remodeling jobs on which the remodeler is carrying the financing until the job is completed.

Use a separate line for each job. Each job will have two (2) lines, one in the Work-In-Progress section and a corresponding one in the Current Liabilities section. Insert additional lines in each category as needed.

Begin by filling in the estimated construction costs in the Job Totals column. For jobs in progress, enter the total amounts completed as of 12/31 of the previous year.

I suggest that you review your past jobs to determine the average percent complete per month and use those percentages to arrive at the monthly amounts for the construction cost. Multiply the estimated total construction cost by the average percent complete per month to arrive at the monthly cost. Use those same percentages to arrive at the monthly draw amount.

Projected Income Detail

The Projected Income Detail worksheet is where you fill in the anticipated Sales and Cost of Sales amounts. Use a separate line for each job. Each job will have two (2) lines, one in the Sales section and a corresponding one in the Cost of Sales section. Insert additional lines in each category as needed.

For one time sales such as the Sale of Land held for Development, the Sale of Developed Lots, and the Sale of Single-Family Speculative homes, enter the total Sales amount and total Cost of Sales in the month in which you anticipate the sale to occur.

For all jobs done on a percentage complete basis, fill in the monthly Sales and Cost of Sales amounts. Start by adding jobs in progress. Then add any pending jobs. Finally, add anticipated jobs.

Begin by filling in the Sales price and the estimated Cost in the Job Totals column. For jobs in progress, enter the total amounts completed as of 12/31 of the previous year.

Again, I suggest that you review your past jobs to determine the average percent complete per month. Multiply the total construction cost by the average percent complete per month to arrive at the monthly Sales amount. Use those same percentages to arrive at the monthly Cost of Sales. For anticipated jobs, if your sales goal is one job per month, use your average Sales price and the anticipated number of months from start to completion and enter the amount of Sales and Cost of Sales using the average percent complete per month.

Line 4000 Indirect Construction Costs, Line 5000 Financing Expense, Line 6000 Sales & Marketing Expense, Line 8000 General & Administrative Expense, and Line 9000 Other Income and Expenses will fill-in automatically from the Indirect Construction Cost and Operating Budget worksheets.

I have entered an Anticipated Job as an example using my typical monthly percentage complete figures.

Indirect Construction Cost

Fill in your projected monthly Indirect Construction Costs.

Operating Budget

Instructions

Fill in you projected monthly Financing, Sales and Marketing, and General and Administrative Expenses.

Projected Cash Flow

Begin by filling in the total End of Period balances from Cash Accounts 1020, 1030, and 1040 in the January Beginning Cash Balance cell. If you maintain an Operating Reserve Account and make regularly monthly deposits to it, fill in those amounts in line 1060. If you anticipate making and Property, Plant & Equipment Purchases during the year, fill in those amounts in the respective months in line 1800. Fill in the projected monthly payment amounts on Lines of Credit in line 2200, the monthly payment amounts on Acquisition and Development Loans in line 2220, the monthly payment amounts on Construction Loans in line 2230, and the monthly payment amounts on Other Notes Payable in line 2290. All of the other monthly amounts will fill-in automatically from the Work-In-Progess, Projected Income Detail, Indirect Construction Cost, and Operating Budget worksheets.

Income Statement - Historical

REVENUE:						
3000	Sales, land held for development					
3050	Sales, developed lots					
3100	Sales, single-family, speculative					
3110	Sales, single-family, production					
3120	Sales, single-family, custom designed					
3125	Sales, single–family, custom, no land					
3130	Sales, residential remodeling					
3133	Sales, commercial and industrial remodeling					
3135	Sales, insurance restoration					
3137	Sales, repairs					
3140	Sales, multifamily					
3150	Sales, commercial and industrial					
3160	Sales, trade-ins and repossesions					
3190	Sales, other					
3360	Construction management fees					
3370	Design fees collected					
3400	Miscellaneous income					
3410	Interest income					
3420	Dividend income					
3450	Earned discounts					
3460	Earned rebates					
	TOTAL REVENUE:	0	0	0	0	0
COST OF SALES:						
3500	Cost of sales, land held for development					
3550	Cost of sales, developed lots					
3600	Cost of sales, single-family speculative					
3610	Cost of sales, single-family, production					
3620	Cost of sales, single-family, custom designed					
3625	Cost of sales, single-family, custom, no land					
3630	Cost of sales, remodeling					
3633	Cost of sales, commercial and industrial remodeling					
3635	Cost of sales, insurance restoration					
3637	Cost of sales, repairs					
3640	Cost of sales, multifamily					
3650	Cost of sales, commercial and industrial					
3660	Cost of sales, trade-ins					
3690	Cost of sales, other					
	TOTAL COST OF SALES:	0	0	0	0	0

INDIRECT CONSTRUCTION COSTS						
4000	Salaries and Wages					
4100	Payroll Taxes and Benefits					
4200	Field Office Expenses					
4300	Field Warehouse and Storage Expenses					
4400	Construction Vehicles, Travel, and Entertainment					
4500	Construction Equipment					
4600	Expenses for Maintaining Unsold Units					
4700	Warranty and Customer Service Expenses					
4800	Depreciation Expenses					
4900	Other					
	TOTAL INDIRECT CONSTRUCTION COST	0	0	0	0	0
	GROSS PROFIT:	0	0	0	0	0
FINANCING EXPENSE:						
5000	Interest					
5100	Construction Loan Points and Fees					
5200	Closing Costs					
	TOTAL FINANCING EXPENSE:	0	0	0	0	0
SALES AND MARKETING EXPENSE: [1]						
6000	Sale Salaries and Commissions					
6100	Payroll Taxes and Benefits					
6200	Sales Office Expenses					
6300	Advertising and Sales Promotion					
6400	Sales Vehicles, Travel, and Entertainment					
6600	Model Home Maintenance					
6700	Sales and Marketing Fees					
6800	Depreciation					
6900	Other Marketing Expense					
	TOTAL MARKETING EXPENSE:	0	0	0	0	0
GENERAL & ADMINISTRATIVE EXPENSES:						
8000	Salaries and Wages					
8100	Payroll Taxes and Benefits					
8200	Office Expenses					
8300	Technology and Computer Expenses					
8400	Vehicle, Travel & Entertainment Expenses					
8500	Taxes					
8600	Insurance					
8700	Professional Services					
8800	Depreciation					
8900	Other					
	TOTAL GENERAL & ADMIN. EXPENSE:	0	0	0	0	0

OTHER INCOME AND EXPENSES:					
9100 Other Income					
9200 Other Expenses					
TOTAL OTHER EXPENSES:	0	0	0	0	0
TOTAL EXPENSES:	0	0	0	0	0
PROFIT / LOSS BEFORE OTHER ITEMS:	0	0	0	0	0
NET INCOME:	0	0	0	0	0

Notes:

Income Statement - Historical

REVENUE:						
3130	Sales, residential remodeling					
3133	Sales, commercial and industrial remodeling					
3135	Sales, insurance restoration					
3137	Sales, repairs					
3190	Sales, other					
3360	Construction management fees					
3370	Design fees collected					
3400	Miscellaneous income					
3410	Interest income					
3420	Dividend income					
3450	Earned discounts					
3460	Earned rebates					
	TOTAL REVENUE:	0	0	0	0	0
COST OF SALES:						
3630	Cost of sales, remodeling					
3633	Cost of sales, commercial and industrial remodeling					
3635	Cost of sales, insurance restoration					
3637	Cost of sales, repairs					
3690	Cost of sales, other					
	TOTAL COST OF SALES:	0	0	0	0	0
INDIRECT CONSTRUCTION COSTS						
4000	Salaries and Wages					
4100	Payroll Taxes and Benefits					
4200	Field Office Expenses					
4300	Field Warehouse and Storage Expenses					
4400	Construction Vehicles, Travel, and Entertainment					
4500	Construction Equipment					
4600	Expenses for Maintaining Unsold Units					
4700	Warranty and Customer Service Expenses					
4800	Depreciation Expenses					
4900	Other					
	TOTAL INDIRECT CONSTRUCTION COST	0	0	0	0	0
	GROSS PROFIT:	0	0	0	0	0

FINANCING EXPENSE:						
5000	Interest					
5100	Construction Loan Points and Fees					
5200	Closing Costs					
	TOTAL FINANCING EXPENSE:	0	0	0	0	0
SALES AND MARKETING EXPENSE: [1]						
6000	Sale Salaries and Commissions					
6100	Payroll Taxes and Benefits					
6200	Sales Office Expenses					
6300	Advertising and Sales Promotion					
6400	Sales Vehicles, Travel, and Entertainment					
6600	Model Home Maintenance					
6700	Sales and Marketing Fees					
6800	Depreciation					
6900	Other Marketing Expense					
	TOTAL MARKETING EXPENSE:	0	0	0	0	0
GENERAL & ADMINISTRATIVE EXPENSES:						
8000	Salaries and Wages					
8100	Payroll Taxes and Benefits					
8200	Office Expenses					
8300	Technology and Computer Expenses					
8400	Vehicle, Travel & Entertainment Expenses					
8500	Taxes					
8600	Insurance					
8700	Professional Services					
8800	Depreciation					
8900	Other					
	TOTAL GENERAL & ADMIN. EXPENSE:	0	0	0	0	0
OTHER INCOME AND EXPENSES:						
9100	Other Income					
9200	Other Expenses					
	TOTAL OTHER EXPENSES:	0	0	0	0	0
	TOTAL EXPENSES:	0	0	0	0	0
PROFIT / LOSS BEFORE OTHER ITEMS:		0	0	0	0	0
NET INCOME:		0	0	0	0	0

Notes:

Projected Balance Sheet

As Of December 31, 20__

CURRENT ASSETS:		
Cash	50,000	
Short Term Investments		
Receivables		
Raw Acreage		
Work-In-Progress Inventory	0	
Finished Units		
Other Capital Assets		
TOTAL CURRENT ASSETS:		**50,000**
NON-CURRENT ASSETS:		
Land		
Buildings		
LESS Buildings Depreciation		
Office Furniture and Equipment		
LESS Furn. And Equip. Depreciation		
Tools and Equipment		
LESS Const. Equip. Depreciation		
Vehicles		
LESS Vehicle Depreciation		
Model Home Furnishings		
LESS Model Home Furn. Depreciation		
Other Capitalized Assets		
TOTAL NON-CURRENT ASSETS:		**0**
TOTAL ASSETS:		**50,000**

CURRENT LIABILITIES:

Customer Payments on Contracts	0	
Accounts Payable		
Notes Payable		
Development & Acquisition Loans Payable	0	
Developed Lot Loans Payable		
Construction Loans Payable	0	
Payroll Taxes Payable		
Unemployment Tax Payable		
Due To Officers and Owners		
Other Current Liabilities		
TOTAL CURRENT LIABILITIES:		**0**

NON-CURRENT LIABILITIES:

Long-Term Notes Payable		
Due to Officers and Owners		
TOTAL CURRENT LIABILITIES:		**0**

OWNER'S EQUITY:

Stock		
Retained Earnings		
Profit and Loss - Year To Date	50,000	
TOTAL OWNER'S EQUITY:		**50,000**
TOTAL CURRENT LIABILITIES AND OWNER'S EQUITY:		**50,000**

Notes:

Projected Income Statement

January 01, 20__ through December 31, 20__

REVENUE:			
Sales, land held for development	0		0.00%
Sales, developed lots	0		0.00%
Sales, single-family, speculative	0		0.00%
Sales, single-family, production	300,000		100.00%
Sales, single-family, custom designed	0		0.00%
Sales, single–family, custom, no land	0		0.00%
Sales, residential remodeling	0		0.00%
Sales, commercial and industrial remodeling	0		0.00%
Sales, insurance restoration	0		0.00%
Sales, repairs	0		0.00%
Sales, multifamily	0		0.00%
Sales, commercial and industrial	0		0.00%
Sales, trade-ins and repossesions	0		0.00%
Sales, other	0		0.00%
Construction management fees	0		0.00%
Design fees collected	0		0.00%
Miscellaneous income	0		0.00%
Interest income	0		0.00%
Dividend income	0		0.00%
Earned discounts	0		0.00%
Earned rebates	0		0.00%
TOTAL REVENUE:		**300,000**	**100.00%**
COST OF SALES:			
Cost of Sales, Land Held for Development	0		0.00%
Cost of Sales, Developed Lots	0		0.00%
Cost of Sales, Single-Family Spec	0		0.00%
Cost of Sales, Single-Family Production	250,000		83.33%
Cost of Sales, Single-Family Custom Designed	0		0.00%
Cost of Sales, Single-Family Custom No Land	0		0.00%
Cost of Sales, Residential Remodeling	0		0.00%
Cost of Sales, Remodeling Commercial and Industrial Remodelin	0		0.00%
Cost of Sales, Insurance Restoration	0		0.00%
Cost of Sales, Repairs	0		0.00%
Cost of Sales, Multi-Family	0		0.00%
Cost of Sales, Commercial and Industrial	0		0.00%
Cost of Sales, Trade Ins	0		0.00%
Cost of Sales, Other	0		0.00%
TOTAL COST OF SALES:		**250,000**	**83.33%**

INDIRECT CONSTRUCTION COSTS			
Salaries and Wages	0		0.00%
Payroll Taxes and Benefits	0		0.00%
Field Office Expenses	0		0.00%
Field Warehouse and Storage Expenses	0		0.00%
Construction Vehicles, Travel, and Entertainment	0		0.00%
Construction Equipment	0		0.00%
Expenses for Maintaining Unsold Units	0		0.00%
Warranty and Customer Service Expenses	0		0.00%
Depreciation Expenses	0		0.00%
Other	0		0.00%
TOTAL INDIRECT CONSTRUCTION EXPENSE:		**0**	**0.00%**
GROSS PROFIT:		**50,000**	**16.67%**
FINANCING EXPENSE:			
Interest	0		0.00%
Construction Loan Points and Fees	0		0.00%
Closing Costs	0		0.00%
TOTAL FINANCING EXPENSE:		**0**	**0.00%**
MARKETING EXPENSE:			
Sale Salaries and Commissions	0		0.00%
Payroll Taxes and Benefits	0		0.00%
Sales Office Expenses	0		0.00%
Advertising and Sales Promotion	0		0.00%
Sales Vehicles, Travel, and Entertainment	0		0.00%
Model Home Maintenance	0		0.00%
Sales and Marketing Fees	0		0.00%
Depreciation	0		0.00%
Other Marketing Expense	0		0.00%
TOTAL MARKETING EXPENSE:		**0**	**0.00%**
GENERAL & ADMINISTRATIVE EXPENSES:			
Salaries and Wages	0		0.00%
Payroll Taxes and Benefits	0		0.00%
Office Expenses	0		0.00%
Technology and Computer Expenses	0		0.00%
Vehicle, Travel & Entertainment Expenses	0		0.00%
Taxes	0		0.00%
Insurance	0		0.00%
Professional Services	0		0.00%
Depreciation	0		0.00%
Other	0		0.00%
TOTAL GENERAL & ADMIN. EXPENSE:		**0**	**0.00%**
OTHER INCOME AND EXPENSES:			
Other Income	0		0.00%
Other Expenses	0		0.00%
TOTAL OTHER INCOME AND EXPENSES:		**0**	**0.00%**
TOTAL EXPENSES:		**0**	**0.00%**
PROFIT / LOSS BEFORE OTHER ITEMS:		**50,000**	**16.67%**

NET INCOME:	**50,000**	**16.67%**

Notes:

Work-In-Progress Detail

Acct.	Job No.	Description	Job Totals	12/31/20__	January	February	March	April	May	June	July	August	September	October	November	December	Year End Totals
WORK IN PROGRESS																	
1410		Land Development Costs [1]															
																	0
																	0
		Total Land Development Costs		0	0	0	0	0	0	0	0	0	0	0	0	0	0
1420		Developed Lots [2]															
																	0
																	0
																	0
																	0
		Total Developed Lots		0	0	0	0	0	0	0	0	0	0	0	0	0	0
1430		Direct Construction Costs [3]															
																	0
																	0
																	0
																	0
		Total Direct Construction Costs		0	0	0	0	0	0	0	0	0	0	0	0	0	0
		TOTAL WORK-IN-PROGRESS		0	0	0	0	0	0	0	0	0	0	0	0	0	0
CURRENT LIABILITIES																	
2010		Contract Deposits [4]															
																	0
																	0
																	0
																	0
		Total Contract Deposits		0	0	0	0	0	0	0	0	0	0	0	0	0	0
2020		Customer Payments on Contract [5]															
																	0
																	0
																	0
																	0
		Total Customer Payments on Contract		0	0	0	0	0	0	0	0	0	0	0	0	0	0
2220		Acquis. & Devel. Loans Payable [6]															
																	0
																	0
		Total Acquis. & Devel. Loans Payable		0	0	0	0	0	0	0	0	0	0	0	0	0	0
2230		Construction Loans Payable [7]															
																	0
																	0
																	0
																	0
		Total Construction Loans Payable		0	0	0	0	0	0	0	0	0	0	0	0	0	0
		TOTAL CURRENT LIABILITIES		0	0	0	0	0	0	0	0	0	0	0	0	0	0

NOTES:

(1). Cost of land and land development, including cost of raw land, financing and interest, land planning, engineering, grading, streets, curbs and gutters, sidewalks, storm sewers, temporary utilities, professional fees, permits and other costs.
(2). Cost of developed lots purchased which have not yet been placed into construction and allocated to individual units under construction.
(3). Direct construction costs, including permits, labor, materials, subcontractors, and any other direct charge during construction.
(4). Down payments, earnest money, and deposits on "Revenue at Job Sale" jobs on which company owns the full assets of the
(5). Customer payments on "Revenue at Job Sale" jobs on which company owns the full assets of the
(6). Draws against land acquisition and development loans.
(7). Draws against construction loans on "Revenue at Job Sale" jobs on which company owns the full assets of the

Income Projection Detail

Acct.	Job No.	Description	Job Totals	Totals as of 12/31/__	January	February	March	April	May	June	July	August	September	October	November	December	Year End Totals	Ratio	Target
Sales																			
3000		**Sales, Land Held for Development**																0.0%	
																	0		
																	0		
																	0		
3050		**Sales, Developed Lots**																0.0%	
																	0		
																	0		
																	0		
3100		**Sales, Single-Family Speculative**																0.0%	
																	0		
																	0		
																	0		
3110		**Sales, Single-Family Production**																100.0%	
	001	Example Anticipated Job	300,000	0	0%	0%	7% 21,000	24% 72,000	21% 63,000	9% 27,000	16% 48,000	23% 69,000	0%	0%	0%	0%	300,000		
																	0		
																	0		
3120		**Sales, Single-Family Custom Designed**																0.0%	
																	0		
																	0		
																	0		
3120		**Sales, Single-Family Custom No Land**																0.0%	
																	0		
																	0		
																	0		
3130		**Sales, Residential Remodeling**																0.0%	
																	0		
																	0		
																	0		
3133		**Sales, Commercial and Industrial Remodeling**																0.0%	
																	0		
																	0		
																	0		
3135		**Sales, Insurance Restoration**																0.0%	
																	0		
																	0		
																	0		
3137		**Sales, Repairs**																0.0%	
																	0		
																	0		
																	0		
3140		**Sales, Multi-Family**																0.0%	
																	0		
																	0		
																	0		
3150		**Sales, Commercial and Industrial**																0.0%	
																	0		
																	0		
																	0		
3160		**Sales, Trade-Ins and Repossesions**																0.0%	
																	0		
																	0		
																	0		
3190		**Sales, Other**																0.0%	
																	0		
																	0		
																	0		
3360		**Construction Management Fee Income**																0.0%	
																	0		
																	0		
																	0		
3379		**Design Fees Collected**																0.0%	
																	0		
																	0		
																	0		
3400		**Miscellaneous Income**																0.0%	
																	0		
																	0		
																	0		
3410		Interest Income															0	0.0%	
3420		Dividend Income															0	0.0%	
3450		Earned Discounts															0	0.0%	
3460		Earned Rebates															0	0.0%	
		TOTAL REVENUE		0	0	0	21,000	72,000	63,000	27,000	48,000	69,000	0	0	0	0	300,000	100.0%	100.0%

Income Projection Detail

Acct.	Job No.	Description	Job Totals	Totals as of 12/31/__	January	February	March	April	May	June	July	August	September	October	November	December	Year End Totals	Ratio	Target
COST OF SALES																			
3500		Cost of Sales, Land Held for Development																0.0%	
																	0		
																	0		
																	0		
3550		Cost of Sales, Developed Lots																0.0%	
																	0		
																	0		
																	0		
3600		Cost of Sales, Single-Family Spec																0.0%	
															0		0		
																	0		
																	0		
3610		Cost of Sales, Single-Family Production																83.3%	
	001	Example Anticipated Job	250,000	0	0%	0%	7% 17,500	24% 60,000	21% 52,500	9% 22,500	16% 40,000	23% 57,500	0%	0%	0%	0%	250,000		
																	0		
																	0		
3620		Cost of Sales, Single-Family Custom Designed																0.0%	
																	0		
																	0		
																	0		
3625		Cost of Sales, Single-Family Custom No Land																0.0%	
																	0		
																	0		
																	0		
3630		Cost of Sales, Residential Remodeling																0.0%	
																	0		
																	0		
																	0		
3633		Cost of Sales, Remodeling Commercial and Industrial Remodeling																0.0%	
																	0		
																	0		
																	0		
3635		Cost of Sales, Insurance Restoration																0.0%	
																	0		
																	0		
																	0		
3637		Cost of Sales, Repairs																0.0%	
																	0		
																	0		
																	0		
3640		Cost of Sales, Multi-Family																0.0%	
																	0		
																	0		
																	0		
3650		Cost of Sales, Commercial and Industrial																0.0%	
																	0		
																	0		
																	0		
3660		Cost of Sales, Trade Ins																0.0%	
																	0		
																	0		
																	0		
3690		Cost of Sales, Other																0.0%	
																	0		
																	0		
																	0		
4000		Indirect Construction Costs																0.0%	
					0	0	0	0	0	0	0	0	0	0	0	0	0		
		TOTAL COST OF SALES		0	0	0	17,500	60,000	52,500	22,500	40,000	57,500	0	0	0	0	250,000	83.3%	70.0%
		GROSS PROFIT		0	0	0	3,500	12,000	10,500	4,500	8,000	11,500	0	0	0	0	50,000	16.7%	30.0%
		OPERATING EXPENSE																	
5000		Financing Expense			0	0	0	0	0	0	0	0	0	0	0	0	0	0.0%	2.5%
6000		Sales & Marketing Expense			0	0	0	0	0	0	0	0	0	0	0	0	0	0.0%	2.5%
8000		General & Administrative Expense			0	0	0	0	0	0	0	0	0	0	0	0	0	0.0%	3.5%
9000		Other Income and Expenses			0	0	0	0	0	0	0	0	0	0	0	0	0	0.0%	5.0%
		MONTHLY NET PROFIT (LOSS)			0	0	3,500	12,000	10,500	4,500	8,000	11,500	0	0	0	0	0		
		CUMM. NET PROFIT (LOSS)			0	0	3,500	15,500	26,000	30,500	38,500	50,000	50,000	50,000	50,000	50,000	50,000	16.7%	16.5%

NOTES:

Indirect Construction Costet

Acct.	January	February	March	April	May	June	2009 July	August	September	October	November	December	Year End Totals
4000–4990 Indirect Construction Cost													
4000–4090 Salaries and Wages													
4010 Superintendents													0
4020 Laborers													0
4030 Production Manager													0
4040 Architects, Drafters, Estimators, Purchaser:													0
4050 Warranty and Customer Service Manager													0
4060 Warranty and Customer Service Labor													0
4070 Other Indirect Construction Wages													0
4100–4190 Payroll Taxes and Benefits													
4110 Payroll Taxes													
FICA - E	0	0	0	0	0	0	0	0	0	0	0	0	0
FUTA	0	0	0	0	0	0	0	0	0	0	0	0	0
MEDC - E	0	0	0	0	0	0	0	0	0	0	0	0	0
SITA	0	0	0	0	0	0	0	0	0	0	0	0	0
SUTA	0	0	0	0	0	0	0	0	0	0	0	0	0
4120 Workers' Compensation Insurance													
Administrative per $100	0	0	0	0	0	0	0	0	0	0	0	0	0
4130 Health and Accident Insurance													
4140 Retirement, Pension, Profit Sharing													
4150 Union Benefits													
4190 Other Benefits													
4200–4290 Field Office Expenses													
4210 Rent, Field Office													0
4230 Field Office, Repairs and Maintenance													0
4250 Utilities, Field Office													0
4260 Telephone, Field Office													0
4265 Mobile phones, pagers, radios													0
4290 Other Field Office Expense													0
4300–4390 Field Warehouse and Storage Expe													
4310 Rent, Field Warehouse and Storage													0
4330 Repairs and Maint., Field Warehouse and !													0
4350 Utilities, Field Warehouse and Storage													0
4360 Telephone, Field Warehouse and Storage													0
4400–4490 Construction Vehicles, Travel, andnment													
4410 Lease Payment, Construction Vehicles													0
4420 Mileage Reimbursement													0
4430 Repairs and Maintenance, Construction Ve													0
4440 Operating Expenses, Construction Vehicles													0
4450 Taxes, Licenses, Insurance, Construction \													0
4460 Travel, Construction Department													0
4470 Customer Business Entertainment, Constru													0
4480 Training and Education, Construction													0
4490 Recruiting Fees and Expenses, Constructic													0

Indirect Construction Costet

Acct.	January	February	March	April	May	June	2009 July	August	September	October	November	December	Year End Totals
4500–4590 Construction Equipment													
4510 Rent, Construction Equipment													0
4530 Repairs and Maintenance, Construction Eq													0
4540 Operating Expense, Construction Equipmer													0
4550 Taxes and Insurance, Construction Equipm													0
4560 Small Tools and Supplies													0
4600–4690 Expenses for Maintaining Unsold U Units under Construction													
4610 Temporary Utilities													0
4620 Trash Maintenance													0
4640 Lawn Care													0
4650 Utilities, Completed Units													0
4660 Repairs and Maintenance, Completed Units													0
4700–4790 Warranty and Customer Service													
4710 Salaries and Wages, Warranty													0
4720 Material, Warranty													0
4730 Trade Contractor, Warranty													0
4790 Other Warranty Expenses													0
4800–4890 Depreciation Expenses													
4820 Depreciation, Construction Office													0
4830 Depreciation, Warehouse													0
4840 Depreciation, Construction Vehicles													0
4850 Depreciation, Construction Equipment													0
4900–4990 Other													
4910 Insurance and Bonding Expenses													0
Total Indirect Construction Costs	0	0	0	0	0	0	0	0	0	0	0	0	0

Operating Budget

20

Acct. Description	January	February	March	April	May	June	July	August	September	October	November	December	Year End Totals
5000–5990 Financing Expenses													
5010 Interest on Lines of Credit													0
5020 Interest on Notes Payable													0
5030 Interest on Developed Lot Loans													0
5040 Interest on Construction Loans													0
5050 Interest of Completed Spec Inventory (1)													0
5090 Interest Expense, Other													0
5100–5190 Construction Loan Points and Fees													
5120 Points and Fees													0
5130 Appraisal and Related Fees													0
5140 Inspection Fees													0
5200–5290 Closing Costs													
5210 Closing Costs													0
5220 Title and Recording Fees													0
5230 Loan Fees													0
Total Financing Expenses	0	0	0	0	0	0	0	0	0	0	0	0	0
6000–6990 Sales and Marketing Expenses													
6000–6090 Sales Salaries, Commissions													
6010 Sales Manager's Compensation													0
6030 Salaries, Sales Personnel													0
6040 Sales Commissions - In House													0
6050 Sales Commissions - Outside													0
6090 Other Sales Office Salaries and Wages													0
6100–6190 Payroll Taxes and Benefits, Sales arting													
6110 Payroll Taxes, Sales and Marketing													0
6120 Workers' Comp. Ins., Sales and Marketing													0
6130 Health & Accident Ins., Sales and Marketinç													0
6140 Retirement, Pension and Profit Sharing, Sal													0
6190 Other Benefits, Sales and Marketing													0
Total Salaries and Benefits	0	0	0	0	0	0	0	0	0	0	0	0	0
6200–6290 Sales Office Expenses													
6210 Rent, Sales Office													0
6230 Repairs and Maint., Sales Office													0
6250 Utilities, Sales Office													0
6260 Telephone, Sales Office													0
6270 Supplies, Sales Office													0
Total Sales Office Expenses	0	0	0	0	0	0	0	0	0	0	0	0	0

Operating Budget

20

Acct.	Description	January	February	March	April	May	June	July	August	September	October	November	December	Year End Totals
6300–6395	**Advertising and Sales Promotion**													
6310	Print Advertising													0
6320	Radio Advertising													0
6325	Television Advertising													0
6330	Internet Fees, Webpage Design and Mainte													0
6340	Brochures and Catalogues													0
6350	Signs													0
6355	Billboards													0
6365	Promotions													0
6370	Agency Commissions													0
6380	Multiple Listing Fees													0
6390	Public Relations													0
6395	Referral Fees													0
	Total Advertising and Sales Promotion	0	0	0	0	0	0	0	0	0	0	0	0	0
6400–6490	**Sales Vehicles, Travel, and Entertai**													
6410	Lease Payments, Sales Vehicles													0
6420	Mileage Reimbursement													0
6430	Repairs and Maintenance, Sales Vehicles													0
6440	Operating Expense, Sales Vehicles													0
6450	Taxes, Licenses, and Insurance													0
6460	Travel, Sales and Marketing													0
6470	Customer Entertainment Expense													0
	Total Vehicle, Travel & Entertainment	0	0	0	0	0	0	0	0	0	0	0	0	0
6600–6690	**Model Home Maintenance**													
6610	Rent or Lease Payments, Model Home Furr													0
6620	Model Home Rent or Lease Payments													0
6630	Repairs and Maintenance, Model Homes													0
6650	Utilities, Model Homes													0
6670	Lawn and Landscaping Care													0
6680	Clean-up, Model Homes													0
6690	Interest on Model Homes													0
	Total Model Home Maintenance	0	0	0	0	0	0	0	0	0	0	0	0	0
6700–6790	**Sales and Marketing Fees**													
6710	Market Research & Consultation													0
6720	Interior Design Fee													0
6770	Recruiting Fees and Expense													0
6780	Training and Education Expense													0
	Total Sales & Marketing Fees	0	0	0	0	0	0	0	0	0	0	0	0	0
6800–6890	**Depreciation**													
6810	Depreciation, Sales Office													0
6830	Depreciation, Sales Vehicles													0
6870	Depreciation, Model Home Furnishings													0
	Total Depreciation Expense	0	0	0	0	0	0	0	0	0	0	0	0	0
6900–6990	**Other Marketing Expenses**													
6930	Sales Concessions													0
6940	Buy Downs													0
690	Other Sales and Marketing Expense													0
	Total Other Marketing Expense	0	0	0	0	0	0	0	0	0	0	0	0	0
	Total Sales & Marketing Expense	0	0	0	0	0	0	0	0	0	0	0	0	0

Operating Budget

20

Acct. Description	January	February	March	April	May	June	July	August	September	October	November	December	Year End Totals
8000–8990 General and Administrative Expens													
8000–8090 Salaries and Wages													
8010 Salaries, Owners													0
8020 Salaries, Officers													0
8030 Salaries, Management													0
8050 Salaries and Wages, Office and Clerical													0
8090 Other General & Admin Salaries and Wage													0
8100–8190 Payroll Taxes and Benefits													
8110 Payroll Taxes													
FICA - E	0	0	0	0	0	0	0	0	0	0	0	0	0
FUTA	0	0	0	0	0	0	0	0	0	0	0	0	0
MEDC - E	0	0	0	0	0	0	0	0	0	0	0	0	0
SITA	0	0	0	0	0	0	0	0	0	0	0	0	0
SUTA	0	0	0	0	0	0	0	0	0	0	0	0	0
8120 Workers' Compensation Insurance													
Administrative per $100	0	0	0	0	0	0	0	0	0	0	0	0	0
Clerical per $100	0	0	0	0	0	0	0	0	0	0	0	0	0
8130 Health and Accident Insurance													
8140 Retirement, Pension, & Profit-Sharing													0
8190 Other Employee Benefits													0
Total Salaries & Benefits	**0**	**0**	**0**	**0**	**0**	**0**	**0**	**0**	**0**	**0**	**0**	**0**	**0**
8200–8290 Office Expenses													
8210 Rent													0
8220 Office Equipment Rental													0
8230 Repairs & Maintenance, Office													0
8240 Maintenance, Office Equipment													0
8250 Utilities, Admin. Office													0
8260 Telephone & Internet, Admin. Office													0
8270 Office Supplies, Admin. Office													0
8280 Postage and Shipping													0
8290 Miscellaneous Office Expense													0
8300–8390 Technology and Computer Expense													
8310 Computer Supplies													0
8320 Leases, Computer Equipment													0
8330 Leases, Computer Software													0
8340 Network and Web Development Expense													0
8350 Maintenance, Computer Equip.													0
8360 Maintenance, Computer Software													0
Total Office	**0**	**0**	**0**	**0**	**0**	**0**	**0**	**0**	**0**	**0**	**0**	**0**	**0**

Operating Budget

20

Acct. Description	January	February	March	April	May	June	July	August	September	October	November	December	Year End Totals
8400–8490 Vehicle, Travel, and Entertainment													
8410 Lease, Administrative Vehicles													0
8420 Mileage Reimbursement													0
8430 Repairs and Maintenance													0
8440 Operating Expense, Vehicles													0
8450 Taxes, Licenses, and Insurance													0
8460 Travel													0
8470 Customer Entertainment Expense													0
8480 Meeting Expense													0
8490 In-House Meeting Expenses													0
Total Vehicle, Travel & Entertainment	0	0	0	0	0	0	0	0	0	0	0	0	0
8500–8590 Taxes													
8510 Sales and Use Taxes													0
8510 Real Estate Taxes													0
8530 Personal Property Taxes													0
8540 License Fees													0
8590 Other Taxes													0
Total Taxes	0	0	0	0	0	0	0	0	0	0	0	0	0
8600–8690 Insurance													
8610 Hazard Insurance, Property Insurance													0
8630 General Liability Insurance													0
8690 Other Insurance													0
Total Insurance	0	0	0	0	0	0	0	0	0	0	0	0	0
8700–8790 Professional Services													
8710 Accounting Services													0
8720 Legal Services													0
8730 Consulting Services													0
8770 Recruiting and Hiring													0
8790 Other Professional Services													0
Total Professional Fees	0	0	0	0	0	0	0	0	0	0	0	0	0
8800–8890 Depreciation Expenses													
8810 Depreciation, Buildings													0
8830 Depreciation, Vehicles													0
8840 Depreciation, Furniture & Equipment													0
8860 Amortization of Leasehold Improvements													0
8870 Depreciation, Computer Equipment													0
8880 Amortization of Organizational Costs													0
8890 Depreciation, Other													0
Total Depreciation Expense	0	0	0	0	0	0	0	0	0	0	0	0	0

Operating Budget

20

Acct.	Description	January	February	March	April	May	June	July	August	September	October	November	December	Year End Totals
8900–8990	**General and Administrative Expense**													
8900	Bad debts													0
8905	Legal Settlement Expenses													0
8910	Contributions													0
8911	Contributions, Political													0
8920	Dues and Subscriptions													0
	HBA Dues													
	20 Club Dues													
8950	Bank Charges													0
8960	Penalties and Other Nondeductible Expense													0
8990	Training and Education Expense													0
	Total General Expense - Other	**0**	**0**	**0**	**0**	**0**	**0**	**0**	**0**	**0**	**0**	**0**	**0**	**0**
	Total General & Administrative Expense	**0**	**0**	**0**	**0**	**0**	**0**	**0**	**0**	**0**	**0**	**0**	**0**	**0**
9000–9990	**Other Income and Expenses**													
9100–9190	**Other Income**													
9100	Income From Partnerships, Joint Ventures,													0
9120	Loss From Impairment Write-Down													0
9150	Gain or Loss on Sale of Assets													0
9190	Other													0
9200–9290	**Other expenses**													
9200	Extraordinary Expenses													0
9300–9390	**Provision for Income Taxes**													
9300	Provision For Federal Income Taxes													0
9320	Provision For State Income Taxes													0
9330	Provision For Local Income Taxes													0
	Total Other Income and Expenses	**0**	**0**	**0**	**0**	**0**	**0**	**0**	**0**	**0**	**0**	**0**	**0**	**0**

NOTES:

Monthly Projected Cash Flow

Acct.	Description	January	February	March	April	May	June	July	August	September	October	November	December
	BEGINNING CASH BALANCE:		0	0	3,500	15,500	26,000	30,500	38,500	50,000	50,000	50,000	50,000
	PROJECTED CASH RECEIPTS:												
2200	Draws on Lines of Credit	0	0	0	0	0	0	0	0	0	0	0	0
2220	Draws on Acquisition & Development Loans	0	0	0	0	0	0	0	0	0	0	0	0
2230	Draws on Construction Loans	0	0	0	0	0	0	0	0	0	0	0	0
	Revenue												
3000	Sales, Land Held For Development	0	0	0	0	0	0	0	0	0	0	0	0
3050	Sales, Developed Lots	0	0	0	0	0	0	0	0	0	0	0	0
3100	Sales, Single Family Speculative	0	0	0	0	0	0	0	0	0	0	0	0
3110	Sales, Single Family Production	0	0	21,000	72,000	63,000	27,000	48,000	69,000	0	0	0	0
3120	Sales, Single Family Custom Designed	0	0	0	0	0	0	0	0	0	0	0	0
3125	Sales, Single Family Custom No Land	0	0	0	0	0	0	0	0	0	0	0	0
3130	Sales, Residential Remodeling	0	0	0	0	0	0	0	0	0	0	0	0
3133	Sales, Commercial and Industrial Remodeling	0	0	0	0	0	0	0	0	0	0	0	0
334	Sales, Insurance Restoration	0	0	0	0	0	0	0	0	0	0	0	0
3137	Sales, Repairs	0	0	0	0	0	0	0	0	0	0	0	0
3140	Sales, Multi-Family	0	0	0	0	0	0	0	0	0	0	0	0
3150	Sales, Commercial and Industrial	0	0	0	0	0	0	0	0	0	0	0	0
3160	Sales, Trade Ins	0	0	0	0	0	0	0	0	0	0	0	0
3190	Sales, Other	0	0	0	0	0	0	0	0	0	0	0	0
3360	Construction Management Fees	0	0	0	0	0	0	0	0	0	0	0	0
3379	Design Fees Collected	0	0	0	0	0	0	0	0	0	0	0	0
3400	Miscellaneous Income	0	0	0	0	0	0	0	0	0	0	0	0
	TOTAL CASH RECEIPTS:	**0**	**0**	**21,000**	**72,000**	**63,000**	**27,000**	**48,000**	**69,000**	**0**	**0**	**0**	**0**
	TOTAL EXPECTED CASH:	**0**	**0**	**21,000**	**75,500**	**78,500**	**53,000**	**78,500**	**107,500**	**50,000**	**50,000**	**50,000**	**50,000**
	PROJECTED CASH REQUIREMENTS:												
	Work-In-Progress												
1410	Land Development	0	0	0	0	0	0	0	0	0	0	0	0
1420	Developed Lots In Inventory	0	0	0	0	0	0	0	0	0	0	0	0
1430	Direct Construction Costs	0	0	0	0	0	0	0	0	0	0	0	0
	Cost of Sales												
3500	Cost of Sales, Land Held For Development	0	0	0	0	0	0	0	0	0	0	0	0
3550	Cost of Sales, Developed Lots	0	0	0	0	0	0	0	0	0	0	0	0
3600	Cost of Sales, Single Family Speculative	0	0	0	0	0	0	0	0	0	0	0	0
3610	Cost of Sales, Single Family Production	0	0	17,500	60,000	52,500	22,500	40,000	57,500	0	0	0	0
3610	Cost of Sales, Single Family Custom Designed	0	0	0	0	0	0	0	0	0	0	0	0
3625	Cost of Sales, Single Family Custom No Land	0	0	0	0	0	0	0	0	0	0	0	0
3630	Cost of Sales, Residential Remodeling	0	0	0	0	0	0	0	0	0	0	0	0
3633	Cost of Sales, Commercial and Industrial Remodeling	0	0	0	0	0	0	0	0	0	0	0	0
3635	Costs of Sales, Insurance Restoration	0	0	0	0	0	0	0	0	0	0	0	0
3637	Cost of Sales, Repairs	0	0	0	0	0	0	0	0	0	0	0	0
3640	Cost of Sales, Multi-Family	0	0	0	0	0	0	0	0	0	0	0	0
3650	Cost of Sales, Commercial and Industrial	0	0	0	0	0	0	0	0	0	0	0	0
3660	Cost of Sales, Trade Ins	0	0	0	0	0	0	0	0	0	0	0	0
3690	Cost of Sales, Other	0	0	0	0	0	0	0	0	0	0	0	0
4000	**Indirect Construction Cost**	**0**	**0**	**0**	**0**	**0**	**0**	**0**	**0**	**0**	**0**	**0**	**0**
	SubTotal - Cost of Construction	**0**	**0**	**17,500**	**60,000**	**52,500**	**22,500**	**40,000**	**57,500**	**0**	**0**	**0**	**0**
5000	**Financing Expense**												
5100	Construction Loan Points and Fees	0	0	0	0	0	0	0	0	0	0	0	0
5200	Closing Costs	0	0	0	0	0	0	0	0	0	0	0	0
6000	**Sales and Marketing Expense**	**0**	**0**	**0**	**0**	**0**	**0**	**0**	**0**	**0**	**0**	**0**	**0**
8000	**General & Administrative Expenses**	**0**	**0**	**0**	**0**	**0**	**0**	**0**	**0**	**0**	**0**	**0**	**0**
9000	**Other Operating Expenses**	**0**	**0**	**0**	**0**	**0**	**0**	**0**	**0**	**0**	**0**	**0**	**0**
	SubTotal - Expense	**0**	**0**	**0**	**0**	**0**	**0**	**0**	**0**	**0**	**0**	**0**	**0**

Monthly Projected Cash Flow

Acct.	Description	Balance as of 12/31/__	January	February	March	April	May	June	July	August	September	October	November	December
1060	Deposits to Operating Reserve Account													
1800	Property, Plant & Equipment Purchases													
2200	Payments on Lines of Credit													
2220	Payments on Acquis.and Develop. Loans													
2230	Payments on Construction Loans													
2290	Payments on Other Notes Payable													
	TOTAL CASH REQUIRED:		0	0	17,500	60,000	52,500	22,500	40,000	57,500	0	0	0	0
MONTHLY ENDING CASH BALANCE:			0	0	3,500	15,500	26,000	30,500	38,500	50,000	50,000	50,000	50,000	50,000

Notes:
(1)
(2)
(3)

APPENDIX D

STANDARD BUSINESS PLAN TEMPLATE

1.0 Executive Summary

- 1.1 Company Information
- 1.2 Financial Performance and Forecasts
- 1.3 Goals
- 1.4 Capital Requirements
- 1.5 Leadership Team
- 1.6 Market Research and Analysis
- 1.7 Target Market
- 1.8 Competition
- 1.9 Product and Service Strategy
- 1.10 Marketing and Sales Strategy
- 1.11 Risks

2.0 Vision, Mission, Core Values, and Unique Selling Proposition

- 2.1 Vision Statement
- 2.2 Mission Statement
- 2.3 Core Values
- 2.4 Unique Selling Proposition

3.0 Company Overview

- 3.1 Legal Structure and Ownership
- 3.2 Company History
- 3.3 Location
- 3.4 Construction Operations
- 3.5 Affiliations
- 3.6 Outside Support

4.0 Market Research and Analysis

- 4.1 Market Research
- 4.2 Market Analysis
- 4.2.1 Industry and Economic Analysis
- 4.2.2 Market Segmentation
- 4.2.3 Markets and Submarkets

4.2.4 Target Market
4.2.5 Main Competitors
4.2.6 Barriers to Entry
4.2.7 Window of Opportunity
4.2.8 Business Risks

5.0 Product and Service Plan

5.1 Product
5.2 Place
5.3 Price
5.4 Services
5.5 Positioning
5.6 Future Products and Services

6.0 Marketing and Sales Plan

6.1 Marketing Plan
6.2 Sales Plan
6.3 Sales and Revenue Forecast

7.0 Operations Plan

7.1 Administration
7.1.1 Staffing
7.1.2 Bookkeeping and Processing Payables and Receivables
7.1.3 Job Costing
7.2 Production
7.2.1 Staffing
7.2.2 Purchasing
7.2.3 Scheduling
7.2.4 Quality Control Plan
7.2.5 SafetyInformation Technology Plan

8.0 Leadership Team and Staffing Plan

8.1 Leadership Team
8.1.1 Leadership Staffing Plan
8.1.2 Leadership Development Plan
8.1.3 Succession Plan (if applicable)

9.0 Goals and Action Plans

9.1 Goals
9.2 Action Plans

10.0 Financial Forecasts and Budgets

10.1 Revenue Projections
10.2 Operating Expense Budget
10.3 Work In Progress Projections
10.4 income or Profit and Loss Statement
10.5 Balance Sheet
10.6 Cash Flow Statement
10.7 Breakeven Analysis
10.8 Pro Forma Assumptions
10.9 Key Ratios

10.10 Financial Analysis and Conclusions
10.11 Capital Requirements
10.12 Use of Funds Statement

11.0 Review Schedule

12.0 Supporting Data Exhibits

Printed in the USA
CPSIA information can be obtained
at www.ICGtesting.com
JSHW062211160823
46609JS00011B/138